R00968 00943

LB
2901
.F58
1993

Fitz, John.

Grant maintained schools.

$33.00

		DATE	

SOCIAL SCIENCES DIVISION
CHICAGO PUBLIC LIBRARY
400 SOUTH STATE STREET
CHICAGO, IL 60605

BAKER & TAYLOR

Kogan Page Educational Management Series

Generating Income for Educational Institutions John Wheale
Grant-Maintained Schools: Education in the Market Place John Fitz,
   David Halpin and Sally Power
Marketing for Schools David Pardey
Teacher Training in Secondary Schools Rowie Shaw
Total Quality Management in Education Edward Sallis

Kogan Page
Educational
Management
Series

GRANT MAINTAINED SCHOOLS

Education in the Market Place

JOHN FITZ

DAVID HALPIN

SALLY POWER

KOGAN PAGE

London • Philadelphia

First published in 1993

Apart from any fair dealing for the purposes of research or private study, or criticism or review, as permitted under the Copyright, Designs and Patents Act, 1988, this publication may only be reproduced, stored or transmitted, in any form or by any means, with the prior permission in writing of the publishers, or in the case of reprographic reproduction in accordance with the terms of licences issued by the Copyright Licensing Agency. Enquiries concerning reproduction outside those terms should be sent to the publishers at the undermentioned address:

Kogan Page Limited
120 Pentonville Road
London N1 9JN

© John Fitz, David Halpin and Sally Power, 1993

British Library Cataloguing in Publication Data

A CIP record for this book is available from the British Library.

ISBN 0 7494 1067 1

Typeset by DP Photosetting, Aylesbury, Bucks
Printed and bound in Great Britain by
Biddles Ltd, Guildford and King's Lynn

Contents

Acknowledgements		7
Introduction		9
1	**Origins and Development of the Policy**	17
	Origins of the policy	18
	Policy objectives	22
	Formulating and implementing opting out	24
	The policy unfolds	28
	Summary and conclusions	31
2	**Patterns of Opting Out**	33
	The scale of opting out	33
	The pace of opting out	34
	Opting out and school closures	35
	The distribution of opting out	38
	Types of GM secondary school	43
	Summary	46
3	**Local Education Authorities and Opting Out**	48
	Breaking the LEA monopoly	48
	Period of consultation	49
	LEAs' actual experience of opted-out schools	52
	Summary and conclusion	60
4	**Headteachers and Opting Out**	61
	Factors influencing a move towards GM status	63
	The advantages of opting out	71

	Opting for a 'traditional' education?	73
	Summary and conclusion	73
5	**Parents, Pupils and Grant-maintained Schools**	**75**
	Diversity, choice and parental participation	75
	Research methods and data set	76
	GM schools: parents and pupils as 'choosers'	77
	GM schools: parents and pupils as 'users'	82
	Summary and conclusion	84
6	**Opting Out and the Education Market**	**86**
	Wellchester and Milltown: two micro-markets	87
	First-choice realization	88
	State and private schooling	91
	School choice and social class	91
	GM status and reputation management	93
	Pupil perceptions of opting out	95
	Summary	97
7	**The Policy's Long-term Implications**	**100**
	Introduction	100
	The 1992 Education White Paper	100
	The White Paper and the future of LEAs	108
	From aptitude to ability?	111
	Issues for parents and governors	112
	Conclusions	115

Appendix 1: Categories of Social Class — 118

Appendix 2: Contact Addresses and Sources of Information — 119

Appendix 3: Glossary of Key Terms — 123

References — 126

Index — 135

Acknowledgements

The research reported in this book was supported for a period of three years (1989–92) by a grant from the Economic and Social Research Council (Award No. R000231899). While this grant provided necessary funding, the research would have been impossible without the help we received at every stage from the schools involved, in particular their headteachers and many of the pupils and parents that use them. We are also indebted to the officers of certain local education authorities and a smaller number of civil servants within the Department for Education for their cooperation. Various politicians, including a former Education Secretary of State and a Minister of State, also helped with our investigation. To all of these people, we offer our thanks.

Stella Scott was the project's secretary from 1990–92, during which time she had, among many other things, the unenviable task of transcribing over 70 hours of audio recordings of interviews. This work was crucial in enabling us to complete the study, and we are grateful for it. We also owe a considerable debt to the Faculty of Education, University of the West of England, Bristol, for hosting the project throughout its duration and for providing excellent facilities. Without the advice and practical assistance of its finance and computer sections, it is difficult to imagine that we would have got this far.

Finally, we wish to thank the *Journal of Educational Management and Administration* for permission to reproduce in Chapter 3 extracts from our article, 'Local education authorities and the grant-maintained schools policy', which it published in 1991 (Volume 19, No.4, pp.233–42).

John Fitz
David Halpin
Sally Power
May 1993

Introduction

Opting out and the great reform of education

Sections 52 to 104 of the 1988 Education Reform Act (ERA) provide the legal basis for a new category of state, or 'grant-maintained' (GM), school. GM schools 'opt out' of their local education authorities (LEAs) and become autonomously incorporated institutions directly funded by central government. All maintained primary, middle and secondary schools are eligible to apply for GM status. The process of 'opting out' is initiated by school governors or a proportion (20 per cent) of parents petitioning the governing body. The outcome of a secret ballot of parents whose children attend the school determines whether an application for GM status goes to the Department for Education (DfE) for the consideration of the Secretary of State.

Freedom from the control of the LEA, however, is only one of the distinguishing features of a GM school. Another is the composition of its governing body which, unlike that of an LEA-maintained school, does not include party political nominees. Its articles of government also provide for powers in relation to admissions, finance and staffing not presently available to an LEA school. A GM school is not only able to petition the Education Secretary directly for a change in character, it can also invest monies, acquire and dispose of property and enter into contracts with staff and other groups and agencies. Indeed, by virtue of its autonomously incorporated status, a GM school has greater flexibility than an LEA school to deploy income, manage its local reputation and employ teachers and other staff.

While schools which opt out represent a special case of educational self-governance, some commentators have suggested that there is an important sense in which the differences between them and LEA-maintained schools ought not to be exaggerated. Deem and Wilkins (1992), for example, argue that because both GM and LEA schools are in receipt of delegated budgets – the former from the central state, the latter from the local authority under the Local Management of Schools (LMS) scheme – they should not be regarded as dissimilar institutions but rather as ones occupying 'different points on the same self-governing continuum'. Furthermore, they suggest that there is nothing to prevent much of the greater degree of autonomy entailed in GM status being offered to schools which remain with their LEAs.

Deem and Wilkins, however, leave themselves open to the objection that, in identifying ways in which GM and LEA-LMS schools are similar, they underplay the significantly different way each type of institution is accountable for educational standards and the use of public funds. Although a GM school is ultimately responsible to the Education Secretary for the quality of education it provides, it is its governing body which has, unlike that of an LEA school, no clear accountability to any democratically elected government, either local or central, which monitors its affairs and confirms policy. Whether this matters much in practice is open to dispute. Wilkins argues elsewhere (1992) that while the governing bodies of LEA-LMS schools include representatives from the local authority, these are usually 'chosen through political party nomination and (often) have only a tenuous link to the local electorate'. Moreover, as is the case with an LEA-LMS school, a significant proportion of the members of the governing body of an opted-out school is directly elected by parents and teachers. To this extent, it could therefore be argued that a GM school is democratically accountable, though in a different way to that of an LEA-LMS school.

Whatever we think of this argument, and it is one we take up specifically in Chapter 7, one thing is clear, namely, that the GM schools policy is central to the present government's current thinking about the future shape and direction of state education. But more than this, the policy's chief purposes – to diversify school provision; to increase competition between schools; and to enhance parental choice – comprehensively resonate with the government's overarching ideological commitment to market-led approaches to the management and delivery of public services.

INTRODUCTION

Analysis, advocacy and opposition

This book, which is based on the findings of a three-year research study of opting out, provides an evidence-based account of the policy's significance and its short and likely medium and long-term effects. In particular, it discusses the policy's origins; the changes made to its administrative detail and character subsequently; its impact on LEAs and particular schools; and its effects on parental choice and children's experience of education.

Because this book is concerned to examine opting out *as a policy*, it does not offer practical guidance on how to achieve GM status, plenty of which is, in any event, available elsewhere (eg, Davies and Anderson, 1992; Nobel and Wright, 1992). Nor does it engage in hostile polemic with the aim of discouraging the process, though Chapter 7 does review a number of issues which governing bodies and parent groups need to bear in mind in considering whether or not to seek GM status for their schools.

While we offer a mostly disinterested account of opting out, the government's support for, and encouragement of, GM status for schools has been full-blooded from start to finish. But, then, so too has the opposition which it has stirred up. Indeed, from the first mention of opting out in the run-up to the June 1987 general election, through discussion of its detail in parliament during 1988, to its subsequent enactment and implementation, the GM schools policy has provoked fierce discussion and aroused strong passions between, and even among, supporters and critics alike.

Certainly the period of consultation about the policy preceding publication of the 1988 Education Reform Bill elicited an avalanche of negative responses (Haviland, 1988). Concurrently, the popular education press published a stream of leaders, reports, short articles and letters about opting out, almost all of which were either directly opposed in principle to GM schools or anxious about their consequences. Many of these expressed concern that opting out would provide a 'back door' route to selective education and a consequent increase in the number of grammar schools (Hunter, 1987). Others commented negatively on its likely effects on LEA planning and finance (Harding, 1987; Meickle, 1987; Sutcliffe, 1987). Some poured scorn on the government's claim that the creation of a GM schools sector would increase parental choice, arguing instead that it would have the undesired effect of exacerbating existing inequalities between different groups of parents and schools (Chanan, 1987; Horn, 1987). To compound matters further, two reported surveys of parents' views indicated ambivalent support for the initiative (Anon, 1988; Thomas, 1987). If that was not enough, various other vested interest groups, representing the voluntary-aided sector, children with special needs and small schools, expressed grave reservations about the likely effects of opting out (Fisher, 1987; Hugill, 1987; Last, 1987; Lodge, 1987; Parkes, 1987). These concerns have persisted and show little sign of abating.

Opting out and 'quality' schooling

The GM schools policy's prominence in government thinking about the future structure of state education is confirmed by the extent to which the 1992 Education White Paper, *Choice and Diversity: A New Framework for Schools* (DfE, 1992a), and the 1993 Education Act, are consolidated around proposals designed to speed up the opting-out process in the hope that by 1995 the majority of secondary schools, at least, will be operating outside the control of LEAs.

With such a policy objective in mind, it is clear that opting out poses a considerable threat to those roles and functions of LEAs which determine the distribution and provision of school places in particular localities. But, then, the government has made no secret of its desire to set these aside in favour of a system in which market forces become the chief arbiter of 'quality' schooling. In fact, lurking behind opting out from the outset has been a deficit view of the work of LEAs, particularly Labour-controlled ones, many of the schools of which have been variously described by the government as inefficient, ineffective and insufficiently accountable. The government argues that opting out will have the effect of promoting the power of the 'consumers' of education (ie, parents) in place of the supposed self-serving vested interests of its 'producers' (ie, LEAs, teachers and educationalists). Moreover, it believes that the conferring of GM status on schools will heighten their accountability and, simultaneously, encourage them to be both more efficient and effective.

The policy's architects also consider that GM schools will contribute to an increase in the diversity of school provision, expand parental choice as a consequence and, through the establishment of new local education markets, encourage an upturn in educational standards, not only within GM establishments, but across private and public school sectors as well. Thus, during the second reading of the Education Reform Bill, the former Education Secretary, Kenneth Baker, defended the GM schools policy as one that 'will improve standards in all schools, not just those which opt out'. Speaking subsequently at the North of England Education Conference in August 1988, he went on to assert that 'grant-maintained schools will be a threat to the complacent and to the second best. They will challenge all within the service to do better'. While this aim has always been writ large in ministerial defences of the policy, the real importance of opting out resides in the questions it raises about the future governance of state schooling and the principles by which education provision is distributed.

Opting out and the reorganization of the public sector

Although this book is solely concerned with the GM schools policy, it is important to note that the principles behind opting out articulate with those underpinning government measures to reorganize other public sector institutions. Speaking at the North of England Education Conference in January 1991, another former Education Secretary, Kenneth Clarke, for example, made explicit a connection between GM status for schools and trust status for hospitals:

> ... the initiative and creative thinking that I wish to see pervading the whole education service is exemplified above all by those schools that go on to seek and achieve grant-maintained status.... The parallel model in the health service is the NHS Trusts. They too are independent of a regional or local tier of administration. I have argued that Trust status would eventually become the 'natural organisational model' for all units providing patient care. I see similar possibilities for grant-maintained status, especially for secondary schools.

Not only has the government encouraged state-funded schools and hospitals to become free-standing institutions; medical general practice and, increasingly, parts of the prison service have also been included in its expanding portfolio of self-managing public sector institutions. Moreover, the recommendations of the Ibbs Report (Efficiency Unit,

1988), which entail many of the executive functions of government being carried out by 'agencies' working to departments of state (Kemp, 1990), indicate that the policy of fostering greater operational decentralization is likely to continue to have a major impact on the control, running and nature of many existing state-funded public utilities and services. As we write, 77 such agencies have been set up, including ones responsible for the Royal Mint, the Public Records Office, Her Majesty's Stationery Office and the Driver and Vehicle Licensing Centres.

Researching opting out

Our examination of opting out, which is restricted to its impact on secondary schooling in England, is based, as already mentioned, upon the findings of a research project we carried out between 1989 and 1992.

The project's research design (Halpin and Fitz, 1990) involved us, sometimes concurrently, in investigations at four levels: within Whitehall and parliament; within LEAs; within individual schools; and within parents' homes. The study as a whole entailed us progressively focusing down from developing a narrative account of the origins and ideological antecedents of the GM schools policy, to examining its impact on the education system nationally, and then to a study of its effects on patterns of educational provision in selected local areas.

We had five concerns at the outset of our investigations:

- To clarify how the GM schools policy was first put together and then taken forward into legislation and subsequently implemented.
- To construct a typology of schools seeking and achieving GM status and to report on the development and nature of the GM schools sector.
- To 'test' empirically the claims and predictions made about the policy by its advocates and critics, in particular those that affect the future role and function of LEAs and emphasize competition between schools within local education markets.
- To report on headteachers' perceptions of the opting-out process and their experience of running a GM school.
- To investigate the degree of parental and pupil support for opting out, including their perceptions of its contribution to choice in education.

INTRODUCTION

These concerns arose out of a set of questions which we were anxious either to answer directly or to throw light on by way of clarification:

- What were the specific problems in education provision which opting out was intended to address?
- What set the policy in motion and why did it take the form and direction that it did?
- What identifiable patterns are there in the kinds of schools which seek GM status?
- What are the motivations behind schools' attempts to become GM?
- What are the perceived benefits and disadvantages of opting out?
- What do parents and pupils think of schools which have opted out?
- What impact do opted-out schools have on their former LEAs and the local systems of school provision they leave behind? In particular, what effects do GM schools have on patterns of choice?

Our research methods included conducting a questionnaire survey of 55 English LEAs directly affected by opting out involving 233 GM schools. Also significant are the on-the-record interviews we carried out with a variety of individuals with differing interests in the policy. Table I.1 shows the number of interviews by category.

Table I.1 *Number of interviews by category*

Ministers and politicians	5
DfE officials	6
LEA officers	24
GM agencies	3
Teachers' representatives	3
GM school headteachers	19
Parents of pupils attending GM schools	106
Pupils in GM schools	264
Headteachers of neighbouring secondary schools	5
Pupils in neighbouring secondary and independent schools	206
Parents using neighbouring secondary and independent schools	51
Other	2

Our research led us to reach six conclusions about the GM schools policy:

- The GM schools policy was loosely conceived at the outset and has been regularly amended since it was first legislated for in 1988 in order to boost its flagging fortunes.
- Because opting out only allows schools to innovate within strict limits and guidelines set down by the government, it has not led to the development of a sector of schools which manifests either distinctive or mould-breaking characteristics.
- Opting out does not eliminate 'producer interests'; rather, it creates a new one in the form of headteacher control which facilitates the policy's implementation and other government education reforms.
- The GM schools policy has had a considerable impact on some LEAs, the planning functions of which have been either inhibited or frustrated entirely by schools threatening to opt out or achieving GM status.
- Opting out contributes little to improvements in parental participation in the life of schools or changes in how children experience education.
- Opting out does not widen parental choice. In some areas where GM status preserves selective education, it may lead to a restriction of choice for parents as a whole.

Summary of contents

This book provides evidence and analysis to support these conclusions. *Chapter 1* outlines the political origins and subsequent development of the GM schools policy. *Chapter 2* interprets some baseline data on the types of school seeking and achieving GM status and reviews the pace and distribution of opting out. *Chapter 3* looks at the early impact of opting out on a selection of LEAs. *Chapter 4* examines the process of opting out through the eyes of 19 headteachers of established GM schools. *Chapter 5* explores the significance of opting out in terms of the perceptions of parents and pupils who use GM schools and adjacent LEA and private schools. *Chapter 6* offers an account of the impact of GM schools in two education 'micro-markets'. *Chapter 7* discusses the likely long-term implications of opting out in the light of the provisions of the 1993 Education Act, in particular for LEAs, and examines some of the issues parents and governors need to bear in mind when considering GM status for their schools.

Chapter 1
Origins and Development of the Policy

Opting out is a policy in motion. Its shifting profile articulates with two aspects of its historical development. First, because it is an enabling, rather than a prescriptive, measure, visible signs of its 'success' depend upon how many schools seek GM status, the number of which has varied considerably from year to year since it was introduced in 1988. Second, since 1988, several significant changes have been made to the administrative detail of opting out. A few of these changes coincide with adjustments in government thinking about the central educational objectives of opting out; the majority with its desire to encourage more schools to become GM. Accordingly, to understand better the nature and significance of the GM schools policy as it operates today, it is important to consider its origins and subsequent development, including its links with government policy generally. Indeed, to write about opting out in ways that focus only on its implications for the mechanics of school governance and the management of school budgets runs the danger of obscuring its ideological and political significance.

This chapter, then, provides a historical analysis of the origins, formulation and subsequent development of opting out. Specifically, it asks and answers three questions:

- what were the conditions which first gave rise to the policy?
- what problems in education was the policy designed to address?
- what changes have been made to the policy during its implementation in the period 1988–92?

In addressing these questions, the chapter draws on a wide range and large number of documentary sources, including party documents and position papers, government publications, and an extensive press cuttings archive. These data are complemented by detailed transcripts of on-the-record interviews with key individuals responsible for developing and implementing the policy (government ministers and other parliamentarians and senior civil servants) as well as representatives of interest groups (teachers' organizations and GM agencies) involved in debating the objectives of opting out and predicting its effects.

Origins of the policy

Following their victory in the 1987 general election, the Conservative government moved quickly to carry out its stated intention to introduce new primary legislation to reform the school system. The result was the 1988 Education Reform Act which contains provisions for the establishment of GM schools to be funded directly by central government grant.

At the time, there was an understandable confusion between the newly proposed 'grant-maintained', and previously abolished 'direct-grant', schools. Direct-grant schools had been fee-paying establishments providing an academic education to selected pupils, many of whose fees were remitted by central government. The 176 schools operating under the old Direct Grant Regulations were required to offer more than 25 per cent of their intake as 'free places' to LEA-nominated pupils who were able to meet their entrance requirements. The Direct Grant Regulations were withdrawn in 1976 by the then Labour government. The majority of the former direct-grant schools continued as independent, fee-paying institutions. GM schools are very different. They cannot charge fees; they may or may not be academically selective; and their grants cover the educational costs of *all* their pupils.

These differences between 'grant-maintained' and 'direct-grant' schools are important because they connect with a lack of clarity about the intended nature of opted-out schools when proposals to introduce them were first given wide publicity in July 1985. Indeed, during a television interview given at the time by the former Prime Minister, Margaret Thatcher, it was made clear that the government was looking again at direct-grant schools (Fairhall, 1985; Passmore, 1985). Subsequent press briefings suggest that consideration was also being given to 'independently owned and run primary schools which would be of high quality and whose aim would be to stimulate schools in surrounding areas to raise standards' (Hodges, 1985). There was also a parallel report in circulation that the former Department of Education and Science (DES) was drawing up plans of its own to establish a network of directly funded and administered 'crown' secondary schools to serve primarily inner-city areas (Flude and Hammer, 1990). As with the primary school initiative, it was envisaged that these schools would act as models of good practice.

The government's desire to 'raise standards' in education and to create 'model' schools as 'beacons of excellence' arose out of its negative assessment of the nature and quality of the work of teachers and education professionals generally. Its critique in this connection was largely fuelled by the arguments of certain New Right pamphleteers, especially the so-called 'Black Paper' authors (Cox and Boyson, 1975, 1977; Cox and Dyson, 1969a, 1969b), who claimed that standards in education had declined because of the abandonment of academic selection and the widespread use of progressive teaching methods in schools. Their case was reinforced during 1976 by the widespread media attention given to the dismissal of the headteacher and most of the staff of a junior school in Islington, all of whom were purported to have abused their autonomy and manipulated the curriculum for ideologically-motivated purposes. The events at William Tyndale Junior School (reported in Gretton and Jackson, 1976) not only encouraged a deficit view of the work of teachers, they also facilitated a form of 'scapegoating' whereby the alleged ills of the education service were regarded as a contributory cause of economic decline. This kind of analysis, it needs to be stressed, was not particular to the New Right. On the contrary, the Labour Prime Minister, James Callaghan, concluded, in the course of a speech made at Ruskin College in October 1976, that education was not sufficiently concerned to prepare students for the world of work.

The context for the emergence of the GM schools policy was not then just a straightforward educational one. True, the government was anxious to remedy alleged deficiencies in the education service through the establishment of new kinds of schools. But it was also concerned, in the wake of a growing fiscal crisis, to implement policies for non-subsidized economic renewal featuring the provision of cheaper and more efficient public services (Dale, 1992; Dearlove and Saunders, 1991). These policies included proposals to deregulate private sector enterprises, reduce the scale of welfare and social policy provision, and 'privatize' public sector institutions. In education, a central concern of the government was to undermine the influence of LEAs, particularly Labour-controlled ones unsympathetic to its policies, and to break down their control of the provision of education services.

During the early 1980s, education policy-making within the Conservative Party thus lay at the confluence of two strands of thinking. For the Black Paper authors and their successors, raising standards in education was to be achieved via the restoration of opportunities for the academically able to attend grammar schools, allied to greater emphasis for all students on the 'basics' of literacy and numeracy. While this was the way forward for many Conservative Party educationalists, there were others, most notably neo-liberals like Stuart Sexton, who argued that standards in education, as well as in other public services, would also be raised if the institutions responsible were compelled to organize and manage their affairs in ways similar to those prevailing in the commercial and business world. The idea behind this shift in emphasis was to encourage less 'producer-dominated' and more 'consumer-orientated' approaches to the provision of welfare. A key assumption was that the distribution of social goods is best effected by competitive markets, much as consumer goods are more efficiently and fairly distributed via the mechanism of free enterprise. On this understanding, LEAs were viewed as bastions of 'producer' vested interests which frustrate competition and stand in the way of progress in education.

To understand fully the reasons behind the emergence of the GM schools policy, we also need to appreciate its resonance with the government's broad electoral commitments in education. Since 1979, successive Conservative administrations wanted to become more directly involved in the details of education provision, including not only the organization of schooling, but the content of the school curriculum as well. This interest arose largely because education was perceived by party managers and manifesto writers as an electorally important area in which the Conservatives might capitalize by amplifying the anxieties of many parents and the ill-founded prejudices of a few.

During the period 1982–6, when Sir Keith Joseph was Education Secretary, the government's desire and willingness to shape the character and direction of education provision became very apparent. The publication of a series of position papers setting out 'good practice' for schools, alongside attempts to tighten central control of the content of teacher education, were clear signs of the government's support for central administrators to intervene directly in matters which they previously had left to LEAs and higher education institutions.

But education was also the focus of successive attempts by central government to develop policies linking expanded parental choice with the creation of new and highly diversified local education markets. This project provided the ideological underpinning for a number of policies, of which opted-out schools can be interpreted as the latest in a series of initiatives to place parents at the centre of educational provision. In this respect, the 1981 Assisted Places Scheme (APS) is important because it was one of the first policies to bring together a number of key elements of Conservative thinking in education.

In providing financial assistance to enable economically disadvantaged pupils to attend academically selective independent schools, the APS was justified on the grounds that it would extend academic opportunities and expand choice to groups which had previously been unable to exercise it fully (Edwards, Fitz and Whitty, 1989). By implication, it advanced the view that state schools were unable to meet adequately the educational needs of the most able pupils, and particularly those living in the inner cities who were considered to be the most likely beneficiaries. Like the direct-grant schools policy, the APS was conceived as 'a ladder of opportunity' for able children from working-class backgrounds. The APS also promulgated, albeit in a very limited way, the important role of markets in education, to the extent that it was designed to provide the opportunity for families to exercise choice across school sectors. It was also one of the earliest signs of the Government's willingness, in times when it was committed to general reductions in state expenditure, to put resources into initiatives which furthered its ideological and political objectives.

More radical proposals to extend choice were made by advocates of the 'educational voucher' who argued that parents should be given the opportunity to exchange the value of their children's education at schools of their choice, including ones in the private sector. In 1982–3, these proposals were given serious consideration by the DES. However, interest in the initiative ceased when an evaluation of a pilot scheme found it to be mostly impracticable. Despite this setback, the educational voucher remains a long-term policy objective for many New Right thinkers in education, of whom Sexton is probably the most outspoken example.

Several factors contributed to the failure of the voucher proposals. On the one hand, there was no evidence to suggest that independent schools were sufficiently interested in becoming involved (Edwards *et al.*, 1989). On the other hand, and more importantly, the funding mechanisms for state schools, which it was envisaged would operate mostly through blocks of money administered by LEAs rather than individual institutions, made the voucher a cumbersome and bureaucratic measure. This weakness in the original scheme explains why, at the time, Sexton was convinced that changing schools into freestanding cost centres was a necessary condition for the introduction of the educational voucher.

It is against this background of limited progress in establishing expanded parental choice in education that we need to see subsequent suggestions from the New Right for a fundamental revision of the principles and organization of education provision. Chief amongst these were sketchily outlined proposals for the establishment of centrally-funded schools operating as charitable trusts independent of LEA control and influence. This idea was developed further and consolidated in a number of pamphlets published by neo-liberal groups of New Right propagandists, most notably The No Turning Back Group of MPs (1986), the Hillgate Group (1986) and the Education Unit of the Institute of Economic Affairs (Sexton, 1987). Alongside ministerial speeches preceding both the 1987 general election and the introduction of the 1988 Education Reform Bill, these publications anticipated the central purposes and implications of opting out. They also identified and elaborated the problems the policy was intended to address.

Policy objectives

As we stressed earlier, the emergence of the GM schools policy needs to be seen in the light of New Right and government hostility to LEAs and other members of the so-called 'education establishment', including academics, civil servants, teacher trainers and teachers' professional associations. Their perceived in-built resistance to change in education was viewed by the New Right as a major obstacle to the sort of market-led school reforms the government was concerned to introduce.

> The fault lies within the heart of the system and that is where the changes must be made. The central feature of our educational system is its complete domination by the producers. Those engaged in the production of education, be they teachers, educational academics, local authority administrators or ministerial civil servants, have an authority over it so complete that the consumer has practically no input (No Turning Back Group of MPs, 1986, pp 8–9).

A similar kind of argument was used by Baker during the course of a speech to the 1987 Conservative Party Annual Conference: 'the smug complacency of too many educationalists has left our national educational performance limping behind that of our industrial competitors'. Baker further argued that, because GM schools would be free from LEA control, they would prove particularly attractive to inner-city parents. In addition, schools that opt out would, he said, 'be a powerful incentive to LEAs to become more responsive to local needs and wishes... What we are introducing to the provision of a public service is competition...'.

The link between market competitiveness, parental responsiveness and the raising of educational standards, on the one hand, and the idea of autonomously incorporated schools, on the other, was also promoted by particular members of the New Right. For example, Sexton, writing at about the same time as Baker's speech, argued:

> that if the system itself were changed to one of self-governing, self-managing budget centres, which were obliged for their very survival to respond to the 'market', then there would be an in-built mechanism to raise standards and change the forms and types of education in accordance with that market demand (Sexton, 1987, pp 8–9).

Sexton concluded that, by pursuing this sort of policy, not only would LEAs become quickly redundant, but so too would the need for an education department of state. The future direction of education would be left instead to the choices of individual parents. This, Sexton concluded, 'is more likely to achieve higher standards more quickly ... than the collective wisdom of the present bureaucrats, no matter how well meaning those bureaucrats may be ...' (Sexton, 1987, p 9).

These arguments are presented in some detail here because they illustrate the shared assumptions about education and its failings held by prominent members of the government and associated New Right publicists prior to the passage of the 1988 Education Reform Act. They also point up commonly-held themes about how to set things right: eliminating 'producer capture' through reducing the power of LEAs and the 'education establishment' generally; empowering new constituencies of parents; and raising standards via competition. Self-governing, autonomously incorporated schools were seen as the chief means of enabling these objectives to be achieved, although, as we indicated earlier, for both the No Turning Back Group and Sexton, the introduction of educational vouchers remained the long-term policy objective.

In the run up to the 1987 general election, however, neither Thatcher nor Baker publicly discussed vouchers as a policy option. Instead, the specific proposals which went forward into the Conservative manifesto reflected the government's intention to enable schools to opt out of LEA control and to receive their funding from Whitehall. These schools, it was argued, would contribute to diversity within the system, which was also to include LEA schools, City Technology Colleges (CTCs), as well as assistance for academically able students to attend, through the APS, selected independent schools.

In education, the government's ideological commitment to 'choice' as the chief principle of regeneration connected with other general populist electoral strategies, including the aim to undermine and eventually nullify the influence of left-wing, 'bureaucratically dominated' metropolitan LEAs. It was also compatible with a range of policies aimed at inner-city residents and council-house purchasers, whose support the government sought to attract and retain (see Gewirtz, Whitty and Edwards, 1992, for a similar comment about the CTC initiative).

Formulating and implementing opting out

The support that opting out received from diverse groups with overlapping membership within the Conservative Party mitigates against any simple interpretation that it had a single author, although both the late Nicholas Ridley, a former (non-education) cabinet minister, and Sexton have claimed to be the policy's prime mover. Without access to the relevant official papers, this matter cannot be settled conclusively;

the key point, however, is that the idea enjoyed Prime Ministerial support which ensured that it became a central plank of the government's overall plan to restructure education.

But how were the political and ideological intentions identified in the previous section translated into specific policy proposals for GM schools? Assisted by the Prime Minister's Policy Unit, and by its head of staff, Brian Griffiths, in particular, the main lines of opting out were put together in the period immediately prior to the publication of the 1987 Conservative Party general election manifesto (Maclure, 1988). Although Baker, as well as some of his officials within the DES, were less than enthusiastic about GM schools, the Prime Minister and other cabinet ministers were committed to them (Ridley, 1992).

The policy taken to the electorate in May–June 1987, however, was somewhat less radical than was hoped for by the New Right. It also lacked detail, sufficiently so for the Prime Minister and her Education Secretary to make contradictory claims about its likely impact (Garner, 1987; Nash and Garner, 1987). While Thatcher, during a press conference, suggested that most schools would want to opt out, and that the policy would also allow schools to become academically selective, Baker, speaking elsewhere, indicated that it would be restricted in its initial impact, and that schools would not be given complete freedom to alter their admissions policies. Baker's interpretation was the one that eventually prevailed.

Shortly after the 1987 general election, the DES issued a series of consultation documents setting out its policy intentions for an anticipated education bill. Issued over the summer vacation, with little time for educationalists to respond, the policies outlined in these documents moved towards the legislative stage with little serious discussion. In Baker's view, speed was important to the success, not only of the GM schools policy, but also other key elements in the Education Reform Bill, most notably the requirement that all state-funded schools should teach and test a prescribed national curriculum. However, one ex-cabinet minister who held office at the time, Ian Gilmour, notes in his memoires that it was 'needlessly provocative and improvident' to press on so quickly with the Bill without properly consulting teachers and other educationalists (Gilmour, 1992). For Gilmour, taking forward the Education Reform Bill was an example of the 'secretive, rushed and highly partisan preparation of legislation during the Thatcher era' (p 194).

As we indicated in the Introduction, the published proposals on opting out were poorly received by the 'education establishment', despite efforts within the DES by civil servants to temper the worst excesses of the keenest advocates of GM status. Although difficult to determine with any precision, it is likely that DES officials were involved very early on in developing the detail of the GM schools policy which they continued to refine throughout the period of the general election. Even so, there are suggestions in our data that, unlike the National Curriculum, opting out was an essentially political initiative that originated outside of the DES (Fitz and Halpin, 1991). As one civil servant closely involved in the early stages of the policy's development put it to us:

> My impression is that (opting out) is very much a policy which came from the politicians which the department was asked to develop. There are two policy routes essentially. Sometimes policies are developed in the department and ministers decide whether they want to run with them, and then ministers themselves have policies. This was a political one that came in on the political side . . . .

It was also initially perceived to be a measure that would offer very little more than LMS, a policy broadly favoured within the DES by the civil service. Consequently, DES officials were concerned from the beginning to ensure that the implementation of opting out would complement rather than frustrate less radical efforts to delegate increasingly more management responsibilities to schools. Indeed, it was at this point in the history of opting out that the considerable influence exerted by officials on the education policy-making process was most in evidence.

DES civil servants had to reconcile the philosophy and differing ambitions of the advocates of opted-out schools, while securing the smooth running of the existing system. What emerged was a policy framework which *enabled*, rather than *encouraged*, schools to opt out of LEA control. The measures relating to opting out in the Education Reform Bill included restricting GM status to schools with 300 places or more, thus excluding most primary schools; funding GM schools at no extra cost to local tax payers and at a level roughly equivalent to that found in LEA schools; restraining the capacity of GM schools to alter their character and change their admissions policies; introducing balloting procedures which not only made it difficult for opting out to take place without proper consultation but gave parents the right to determine the future status of their children's schools; and requiring GM schools to teach the National Curriculum and adopt common articles of governance. In effect, these administrative details both determined the pace at which the policy would eventually be taken up and spelt out the nature of the limited autonomy opted-out schools would enjoy.

As we previously stressed, the measures were rather more conservative than the New Right's preferred proposals insofar as the size restriction limited the number of schools which could consider opting out, while the curriculum constraints meant that individual GM schools could not devise innovative programmes of study and thus market their reputations in distinctive ways. Indeed, although Baker viewed GM schools as 'beacons' of excellence, they were not, unlike their counterparts in the USA or on the Continent, and unlike the CTCs in England, envisaged as centres of innovation. On the contrary, the chief principle underpinning the policy's administrative framework was that the differences between GM and LEA schools were to be minimal so as to demonstrate that the *managerial efficiencies* arising out of institutional autonomy were all that are required to increase standards in schools. As another of our civil servant respondents observed:

> ... people ought to make the choice (to try for GM status) for the right reason, namely, that they are ready for independence; that they are willing to take responsibility for running the school; that they are not doing it for the money; that they are doing it because they think they can improve education with the same sort of resources as the LEA provides.

In devising the policy, officials were also sensitive to its financial implications. Certainly, both the restrictions on the number of schools entitled to opt out and the funding arrangements based on the principle of parity of resourcing for GM and LEA schools were drafted with an eye on the likely negative response by the Chancellor to any sudden increase in education expenditure resulting from an avalanche of successful applications for GM status. If that had been allowed to happen, one official predicted: 'the Treasury would have gone berserk because it would have been overwhelmed by us demanding more cash...'

The fact that over 50 clauses are devoted to opting out in the Education Reform Act indicates the constitutional difficulties officials had to address in devising a legislative framework for a new kind of state school. These difficulties included finding a way to transfer particular assets to GM schools from their former LEAs and establishing rules pertaining to their reallocation should an opted-out school become unviable. There was also a need to take account of the ambiguous position of the Education Secretary and DES officials in relation to opting out. The quasi-judicial role the Education Secretary assumes when assessing the merits of particular applications for GM status articulates uncomfortably with her or his political concern to promote opting out. In effect, because of a clash of interests, neither ministers nor officials can advise individual schools directly about the merits, or otherwise, of seeking GM status. Under the direction of Steve Norris, a Conservative MP, and probably at the request of Baker (Rogers, 1992), the Grant Maintained Schools Trust was therefore established in 1988 to promote opting out and to advise schools about the application procedures for GM status. The Grant Maintained Schools Trust (now Grant-Maintained Schools Centre) receives funds from the government to support its activities. Its initial grant of £25,000 in 1988/9 was expanded in 1991–2 to £600,000. Interpreted by opposition politicians as no more than a 'Tory front' (Hackett, 1993; Judd, 1993), the Centre has been an important adjunct in getting the policy off the ground.

The policy unfolds

Since the first opted-out school opened in September 1989, the GM schools policy has undergone a number of modifications. Many of these adjustments relate directly to government concerns about the pace of the policy's take up, as measured by the number of schools opting out. Although it can be argued that this is a very narrow interpretation of the policy's impact on education, it is the measure which the government has been most often forced to deploy when asked to demonstrate the policy's success. However, it is on such occasions that ministers have clearly felt most vulnerable, chiefly because the number of schools which opt out provides a litmus paper-like test of the popularity of the government's general aim to empower parents as consumers of education. It is in this light that the successive changes in the policy's administrative details must be viewed.

In general, there has been a gradual drawing back from the principle

Table 1.1 *Capital allocations for GM schools, 1990–1994*

Year	Eligible schools	Named project allocation	No. schools	Total allocation (£mill)
1990–91	29	5.8	25	6.3
1991–92	56	8.4	28	10.5
1992–93	102	15.2	50*	28.5
1993–94	337	47.5	215	77.0

* figures include Technology Schools Initiative awards to GM schools
Source: DES & DfE News Bulletins

of minimizing the differences between GM and LEA-maintained schools. The first clear indication of this trend came in January 1990, with the preferential funding made available to GM schools for capital projects. Twenty-nine GM schools were allocated £6.3 million compared with £410 million made available for similar purposes to the country's 24,000 other schools. In 1991, then, a very small number of GM schools received a disproportionately high amount of public money to support their work. As Table 1.1 illustrates, this trend has continued up to the present day. Indeed, the Chancellor's November 1992 Autumn Financial Statement indicates that roughly one-third of the £1.8 billion the government expects to devote to school capital expenditure in the next three years will be directed to schools within the GM sector. Some commentators on opting out have suggested that comparisons between levels of capital expenditure on GM and LEA schools indicate that the former enjoy between two and four times more financial support than their local authority counterparts (Bush and Coleman, 1992; Rogers, 1992).

Other administrative changes have further confirmed the funding advantages of GM status, despite Baker's claim, made in 1988, that the 'effect of opting out should be broadly neutral for both school and LEA'. The introduction of an administratively convenient unified figure with which to calculate the proportion of the LEA central services budget allocated to GM schools calls into serious question the suggestion that there exists parity of funding between GM and LEA schools. Moreover, by determining that opted-out schools should receive, as their proportion of central service costs, an additional sum based on 16 per cent (now 15 per cent) of their former LEA's pupil-based formula, the government made it possible for an LEA to have its central service budget seriously depleted if significant numbers of large secondary schools became GM. Looked at in the light of this possible outcome, it is impossible now to claim, after Baker, that opting out is neutral, either in respect of schools or LEAs.

Other modifications have further dismantled the policy framework in operation at the time the first GM schools opened. At the Conservative Party Conference in 1990, Baker's successor as Education Secretary, John MacGregor, disclosed that he intended to lift the size limit on schools which could seek GM status, thus providing an opportunity for all primary schools to opt out. At the same time, he announced a 50 per cent increase in both the transitional and annual specific grants payable to GM schools. On incorporation, all GM schools would receive a one-off payment of £30,000, plus £30 per pupil, up to a ceiling of £60,000. These measures were interpreted by critics as a blatant financial bribe aimed at bolstering the policy's flagging fortunes. In the short term, they certainly had the effect, as we report in more detail in the next chapter, of increasing the numbers of schools seeking to opt out.

The shift in emphasis, from providing an opportunity for schools to opt out, to positively encouraging them to do so, was confirmed by Thatcher's successor as Prime Minister, John Major, in a letter to the National Union of Teachers in August 1991:

> We have made no secret of the fact that grant-maintained schools get preferential treatment in allocating grants to capital expenditure. We look favourably at GM schools to encourage the growth of that sector and I am delighted to see that numbers are growing rapidly (quoted in Bates, 1991).

This change in the policy's direction was accompanied by a corresponding modification in the way in which ministers justified the extra funding for GM schools. For instance, John Patten, the Education Secretary at the time of writing, defends the policy of providing extra resources to GM schools by referring to the additional burden of responsibilities they assume once they leave LEA control.

There is also increasing evidence that the GM schools policy has become a vehicle with which the government has been able to take forward other educational initiatives. In some cases this has involved changes in emphasis to the intitial policy. The original restrictions preventing GM schools from changing their character made sure that opting out did not foster an increase in the number of selective secondary schools. However, the government is increasingly employing the policy to encourage specialization within the secondary sector. The clearest example of this trend is the favourable treatment received by GM schools under the Technology Schools Initiative (TSI). Intended to enable schools to enhance their provision for technology-related subjects, GM and voluntary schools have been allocated 40 per cent of the TSI budget. This development is further enhanced by proposals to establish GM Technology Schools.

Using GM schools to foster greater specialization is confirmed too by a recent DfE ruling that a boys' comprehensive school in Bromley will be able to select up to 10 per cent of its pupils on the basis of musical or sporting aptitude (Blackburne, 1992). Although this represents only a modest proportion of the school's intake, the larger significance lies in the DfE's determination that such changes in admissions policy, which create a new market in specialist schools, can be undertaken within present legislation and without recourse to lengthy statutory procedures. This opens the door for other GM schools to adjust their admissions policy with the minimum of central regulation. Moreover, the 1992 Education White Paper (DfE, 1992a), and other statements by Patten, indicate that this is a development the government wishes to encourage. There are signs as well that it is now prepared to consider sympathetically requests from GM secondary comprehensive schools to introduce academic tracks involving selection by ability (Hackett and Whitehead, 1993; Hughes, 1993).

Summary and conclusions

At the beginning of this chapter we described opting out as 'a policy in motion', by which we meant to draw attention to the fact that it has undergone considerable amendment both since its promulgation in the run up to the 1987 general election and its subsequent embodiment in the 1988 Education Reform Act. In particular, we have stressed the way in which the policy has changed from originally providing a framework to enable schools to opt out to one in which schools are now actively encouraged to seek GM status. We have also tried to show that, while it was first envisaged that opted-out and LMS schools would enjoy parity of funding and esteem, this principle has been abandoned to the point where the government is now committed to GM status as the predominant model of education governance and provision.

We believe that the changes made to the administrative detail of the policy had several sources. The slow take up of the policy, as measured by the number of schools seeking to opt out, certainly brought problems of legitimation. In response, successive Education Secretaries provided incentives for schools to seek GM status, including the lifting of the size limit on establishments which could opt out and preferential financial support for those that did. These incentives need to be seen alongside the government's determination that LEAs will have a greatly diminished role in an education system dominated by opted-out schools.

The GM sector has also become a convenient conduit for the government to introduce other initiatives in education, notably specialization and selection by aptitude, and to reintroduce old ones, such as academic tracking. Organizationally, GM schools allow the government to by-pass the inconvenient objections of LEAs and national teachers' associations through school-by-school dissemination of its policies, a theme to which we shall return in our discussion of headteachers and opting out in Chapter 4.

The government's resolve to drive opting out forward, despite the manifest difficulties associated with its implementation, is explained in large measure by the compatibility between the policy's central features and the ideological and political commitments of successive Conservative administrations. In particular, opting out simultaneously offers the prospect of increasing choice in education and satisfying groups within society whose support the Conservatives wish to attract and retain. For these reasons, education ministers have been prepared to adjust and amend the details of opting out and, ultimately, to promote it as the flagship of educational reform. Their 'success', measured in terms of the number, type and distribution of schools seeking GM status, is the subject of the next chapter.

Chapter 2
Patterns of Opting Out

The identification of patterns of opting out is important, not only for assessing the overall impact of the GM schools policy, but also for predicting the directions along which the identity of the GM sector is likely to be constructed. In this chapter, therefore, we provide some baseline data on the scale of opting out; interpret the pace at which the policy has been taken up since the passage of the 1988 Education Reform Act; analyse the reasons why some schools sought GM status; examine the distribution of these schools; and report on the type and number of secondary schools which make up the GM sector.

The scale of opting out

At the beginning of 1993, 836 schools had embarked on the process of opting out. Of this total, 337 were operating as GM schools, with a further 26 having been approved by the Secretary of State. Two hundred and twenty-three schools had received positive ballot results from parents; of these, 143 had published proposals for GM status, while 80 were in the process of preparing their applications. Seventeen schools had initiated 'going GM', but the parental ballot was still underway. In 181 cases, parents had voted against their school opting out. The Secretary of State had rejected applications for GM status from 52 schools.

As can be seen from Table 2.1, a broad range of establishments have opted out, from primary schools to sixth-form centres.

Table 2.1 *Progress of the GM schools policy (January 1993)*

	Primary	Middle	Secondary	Tertiary	Total
Operating	65	16	255	1	337
Approved	4	1	21	0	26
Proposals published	28	6	109	0	143
'Yes' vote	27	3	50	0	80
Ballot pending	5	0	12	0	17
'No' vote	44	13	123	1	181
Rejected	19	4	29	0	52
Total	192	43	599	2	836*

(Based on DfE statistical memorandum, 5 January 1993)

*This total includes 11 schools which have embarked on the process of opting out twice, having either been rejected by the Secretary of State or having received a negative ballot result from parents the first time round.

At the time of writing, the total number of establishments that have achieved GM status falls far short of Thatcher's confident assertion in 1988 that most schools would, sooner rather than later, want to leave their LEA. However, while the GM sector includes a very small proportion of all maintained schools (currently less than 1.5 per cent), its significance should not be underestimated. Its impact on secondary provision in particular has been quite considerable. For, although the 65 GM primary schools and 16 GM middle schools constitute only 0.35 per cent and 1.5 per cent of state provision respectively, the GM secondary sector accounts for 7.4 per cent of all state secondary schools. Indeed, as of January 1993, 17 per cent of maintained secondary schools had embarked on the opting-out process.

These crude figures, however, tell us little about the pace of the policy's uptake, the distribution of GM schools, or the reasons why they opt out.

The pace of opting out

The previous chapter highlighted the manner in which the GM schools policy was amended and modified by the government as a consequence of its flagging fortunes and poor uptake. These modifications were influenced by, and are reflected in, the different rates of opting out between 1988 and 1993.

While there were over 50 ballot declarations in the first six months (November 1988 to April 1989), the number reduced to a slow trickle (58) in the following year and a half (see Figure 2.1). The slackening of interest in 1990 may have had something to do with natural cautiousness on the part of many schools which preferred to bide their time and await the outcome and financial implications of local policies for LMS. Others might have wanted to monitor the progress of the first wave of opted-out schools before taking the decision themselves to seek GM status. In any event, the financial benefits of opting out were not just unclear in the first two years of the policy's implementation, they were repeatedly denied by ministers and officials, which may explain why the first wave of schools to seek GM status underplayed its resource implications, emphasizing instead its role in thwarting LEA reorganization plans. Another factor which could have inhibited some schools was the possibility of an early general election and the installation of a Labour government committed to removing GM status from the statute book and returning existing opted-out schools to LEA control.

At the end of 1990, however, there was an increase in interest, which was sustained at relatively high levels during both 1991 and 1992. It is likely that the noticeable upsurge in opting out in the late months of 1990 and throughout the following year, stems from the waiving of the 300-pupil limit and the increased financial incentives announced by the government in October 1990. That the new financial arrangements affecting GM status encouraged an increasing number of schools to opt out in 1991 is evident from data obtained from our questionnaire survey of LEAs (see Figure 2.2). Although the survey reveals that between 1988 and 1991 independence of LEA control was perceived as a significant factor influencing approximately one-fifth of schools seeking to opt out, the desire to obtain preferential funding was mentioned much more often. Moreover, the survey indicates that, in 1991, financial advantage was considered to be more important than any other reason for schools wanting to opt out.

Opting out and school closures

Does this mean then that financial considerations constitute the chief

GRANT-MAINTAINED SCHOOLS

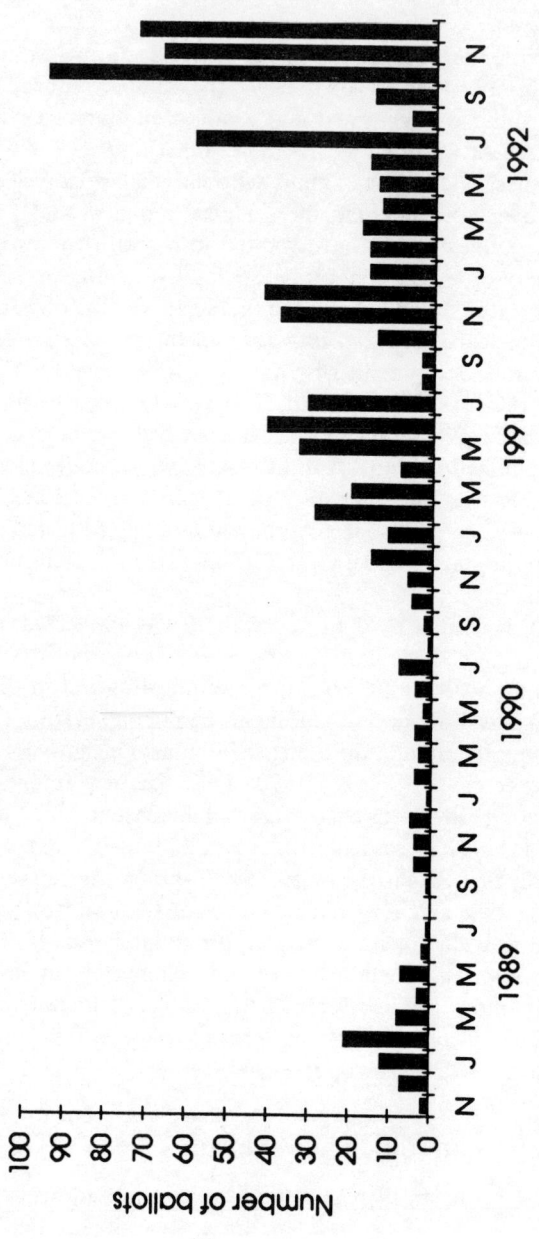

Figure 2.1 *Frequency of ballots since November 1988*

PATTERNS OF OPTING OUT

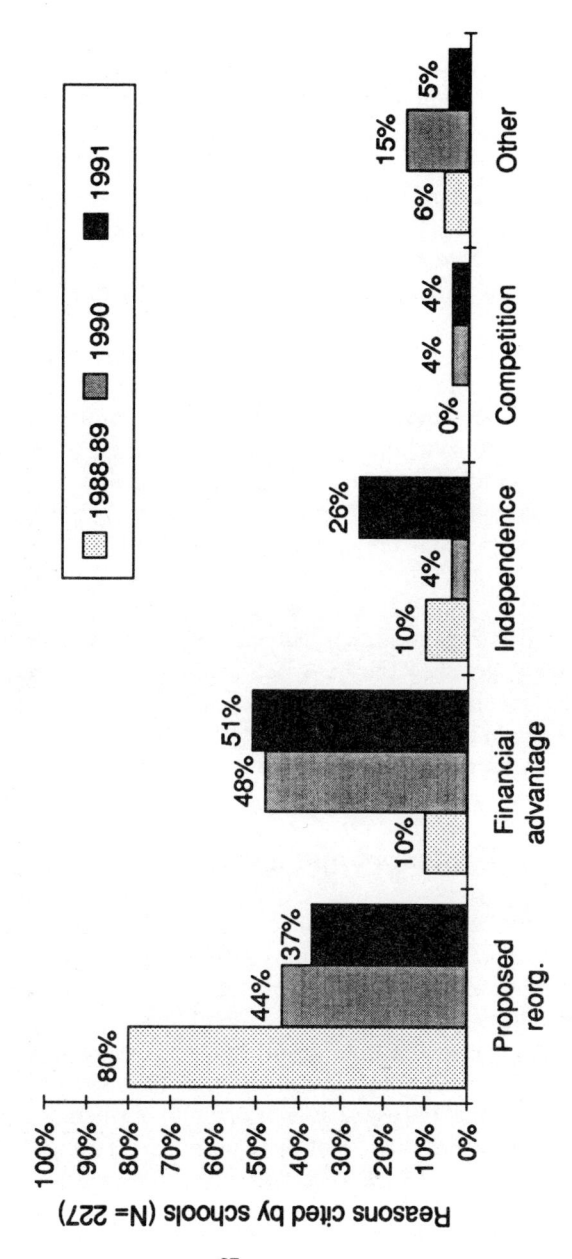

Figure 2.2 *Reasons cited by LEAs for schools seeking to opt out*

reason for schools wanting to opt out? Clearly they are important. But they are not the only influential factor, and in some cases, particularly when a school's future is threatened by its LEA, the issue of finance may hardly figure at all; what matters most is to survive.

But the argument that an opted-out school is more often than not one which seeks GM status to frustrate an LEA reorganization plan has been challenged by the policy's supporters. They point up the fact that a very small proportion of schools which seek GM status do so against the background of a Section 12 or 13 proposal, that is a specific request by an LEA to the Secretary of State to either close or redesignate a school.

However, it is clear from our questionnaire data that many more schools, and far more than the policy's supporters appear willing to acknowledge, opt out to avoid the possibility of closure or redesignation. For those schools for which we have data, nearly a half (107/227) were identified by their LEAs in connection with reorganization schemes, even though they were not necessarily subject to a Section 12 or 13 proposal at the time of the parental ballot. This indicates that probably a greater proportion of schools than has hitherto been thought try for GM status because they think their futures are, or may be, under threat as a consequence of being included in plans provisionally agreed by the LEA but awaiting confirmation in the light of local consultation. In other words, such schools, rather than wait to be included in a Section 12 or 13 proposal, kill the reorganization plan at its inception by seeking GM status.

The distribution of opting out

While alterations to the policy can be used to interpret the changing pace of opting out, they cannot account for the uneven distribution of GM schools. After all, nearly all LEAs are faced with the dilemmas of reorganizing provision and closing schools.

Although, at the time of writing, over four-fifths of the LEAs in England (89/108) contain schools that have sought GM status, and more than half (60) have at least one school where the change in status has been agreed, only 28 of these authorities have more than two GM schools. Indeed, 19 LEAs contain no schools which have sought to opt out.

PATTERNS OF OPTING OUT

The geographical spread of GM schools is one of opting out's more curious features. As the map (Figure 2.3) indicates, some areas of England, particularly the North East and South West, have hardly been touched by the policy. There is a concentration of GM schools in the North West, and in the South East and East Anglia in particular. There are, though, notable exceptions. While Kent and Essex together contain 80 GM schools, the neighbouring counties of Suffolk and East and West Sussex have not one between them. On the other hand, the metropolitan areas of Greater London and the West Midlands contain large numbers of GM schools. In one sense this is hardly surprising given the high density of population in these areas, but it does not explain differences within them (for instance, Ealing has seven opted-out schools, while nearby Harrow has none). Neither does it explain the scarcity of GM schools in other metropolitan areas such as Merseyside and South Yorkshire, each of which has only one GM school.

The prediction that, if one school opts out, this will have a 'domino effect' on others in the same area has been borne out in practice. Of the first 60 LEAs to 'lose' a school to the GM sector, 25 had four or more opted-out schools operating within their boundaries by the beginning of 1993. At the time of writing, six local authorities (Essex, Gloucestershire, Kent, Lincolnshire, Norfolk and Surrey) account for more than 40 per cent of *all* opted-out schools.

While the distribution of GM schools provides one indicator of the impact of opting out, it is also necessary to consider the proportion of schools within an LEA which have left its control. We calculate that 43 LEAs are in the process of 'losing' over 10 per cent of their secondary schools. In 24 cases the proportion of secondary schools where parents have voted to leave LEA control is on or above one-fifth (see Table 2.2). Furthermore, in 12 local authorities, over one-third of their secondary schools have opted out. In four London boroughs, Hillingdon, Bromley, Sutton and Wandsworth, this figure is at least one half.

The numbers of schools involved vary substantially. In Kensington, for instance, the loss of 20 per cent of its secondary schools is accounted for by just one of its schools opting out, compared with the 12 schools which constitute an equivalent proportion of Surrey's provision. Despite these variations, it is the percentage, rather than the number, of GM schools which is likely to be most significant.

These figures also reveal that the government was wrong to expect that the first schools to opt out would be from Labour-controlled

GRANT-MAINTAINED SCHOOLS

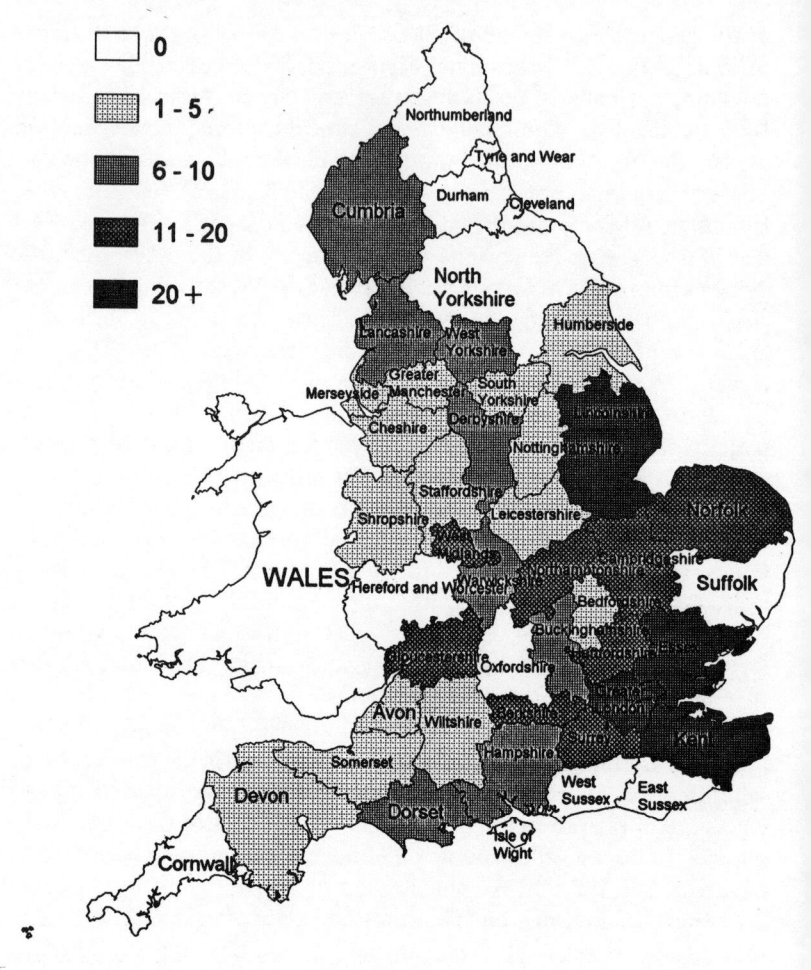

Figure 2.3 *Distribution of GM schools in England, January 1993*

LEAs (see Table 2.3). Only 13 per cent of the 386 schools whose transfer to GM status had been agreed at the time of writing are in Labour areas, while Conservative councils in the shire counties have been amongst those most affected. In fact, two-thirds of approved GM schools are in Conservative-led authorities.

The contrasting rates of opting out in Labour and Conservative

Table 2.2 *LEAs in the process of losing at least 20 per cent of their secondary schools through opting out (January 1993)*

LEA	No. of GM schools*	Total no. of schools †	Percentage loss to GM sector
Hillingdon	11	18	61
Bromley	11	19	58
Sutton	8	14	57
Wandsworth	6	12	50
Essex	46	108	43
Gloucestershire	18	43	42
Lambeth	4	10	40
Kingston-upon-Thames	4	10	40
Brent	6	15	40
Ealing	5	13	38
Lincolnshire	24	64	38
Kent	47	139	34
Cambridgeshire	13	45	29
Bedfordshire	8	31	26
Southwark	4	16	25
Northamptonshire	10	42	24
Calderdale	4	17	24
Cumbria	10	44	23
Norfolk	12	56	21
Surrey	12	58	21
Warwickshire	8	39	21
Wolverhampton	4	20	20
Kensington	1	5	20
Dorset	8	41	20

* Including schools which received a positive parental ballot, but where GM status has not yet been approved, as well as schools already approved and operating.

† As reported by the DES, January 1990

LEAs are not easy to explain. The government's supporters argue that the relatively low number of parental ballots in Labour areas has been influenced by the amount of misinformation on opting out put out by council officials. While undoubtedly some LEAs, including presumably Conservative ones as well, have publicly protested about opting out,

Table 2.3 *GM schools and LEA affiliation* (January 1993)*

	Conservative	Labour	Lib Dem	No overall control
Open and approved	240	46	7	70
'No' vote	66	71	1	43
Rejected	29	11	0	12
Embarked	458	172	10	196

* LEA affiliation is taken at the time of the parental ballot. In seven cases (Calderdale, Dudley, Lambeth, Liverpool, Rochdale, Walsall and Wolverhampton) the originating LEA has changed affiliation.

their actions surely cannot adequately account for the unevenness of the policy's impact nationally. Other explanations which have been put to us by the policy's advocates include claims that headteachers in Labour LEAs are 'political' appointees and will therefore hinder moves to GM status, and even that parents in such areas have been more exposed to the 'dependency culture' of the political Left. Certainly, as Table 2.3 shows, parents in these authorities are far more likely to return a negative ballot result. But this can as easily be interpreted as a vote of confidence in an LEA as it can be said to demonstrate a 'dirty tricks' campaign.

Another explanation is that the rate of opting out is higher in local authorities where the school-based funding per pupil is significantly below the national average. Lower-spending authorities also tend to be Conservative controlled. This interpretation certainly could be made to apply in at least two cases. In 1990–91, Kent, which at the time had the second highest number of GM schools, spent the least amount of money per secondary pupil of all the LEAs in England. In the same year, Lincolnshire, which had the third largest number of schools to have opted out, was ranked 101/108 in terms of the amount it spent per pupil. But the correlation between low spending per pupil and the level of opting out is not strong in every case. For instance, Essex, which has in its area the largest number of GM schools, is not an authority with a reputation for low spending on education. Moreover, Hillingdon LEA, while it is in the top ten of education spenders, has still managed to 'lose' 11 of its schools to opting out. On the other hand, some low-spending authorities, like Leeds, Northumberland and Bury, contain no schools which have sought GM status.

Ranson (1991) has suggested that certain structural and cultural characteristics of a local educational system (for example, if it is managed as an integrated, interdependent whole; if it encourages partnership and collaborative working) may make it less vulnerable to opting out. In this connection, the manner in which the education service in Kent is managed by relatively autonomous district offices may account for the high incidence of opting out in that part of the country. Again, though, it is doubtful whether this argument can be equally applied to the other most severely affected LEAs.

Types of GM secondary school

While it is hard to establish any simple explanation for the geographical distribution of GM schools, it is less difficult to account for the changing patterns in the kinds of schools which opt out. The waiving of the 300-pupil rule in late 1990, for instance, is clearly reflected in the subsequent patterns of uptake. Certainly, the proportion of opted-out primary schools increased dramatically during 1991 and 1992 (see Figure 2.4).

Currently, primary schools make up 19 per cent of the GM sector. Despite this increase, and as mentioned earlier in this chapter, the policy retains its greater significance for secondary education, both in terms of numbers and ministerial pronouncements and projections.

It is also possible to identify trends in uptake within the GM secondary sector itself. Of the first wave of GM schools operating in September 1989, nearly one half (47 per cent) had selective admissions policies. While the rate of grammar schools opting out has remained fairly consistent (see Figure 2.5), that of comprehensive schools has increased. Despite the increase in the number of GM comprehensive schools, in January 1993, nearly a quarter (23 per cent) of the secondary schools in the GM sector were academically selective, a far higher proportion than that found in the LEA sector, within which only 4 per cent of secondary schools were selective prior to the GM schools policy. It is unlikely, though, that this high representation will continue as the

GRANT-MAINTAINED SCHOOLS

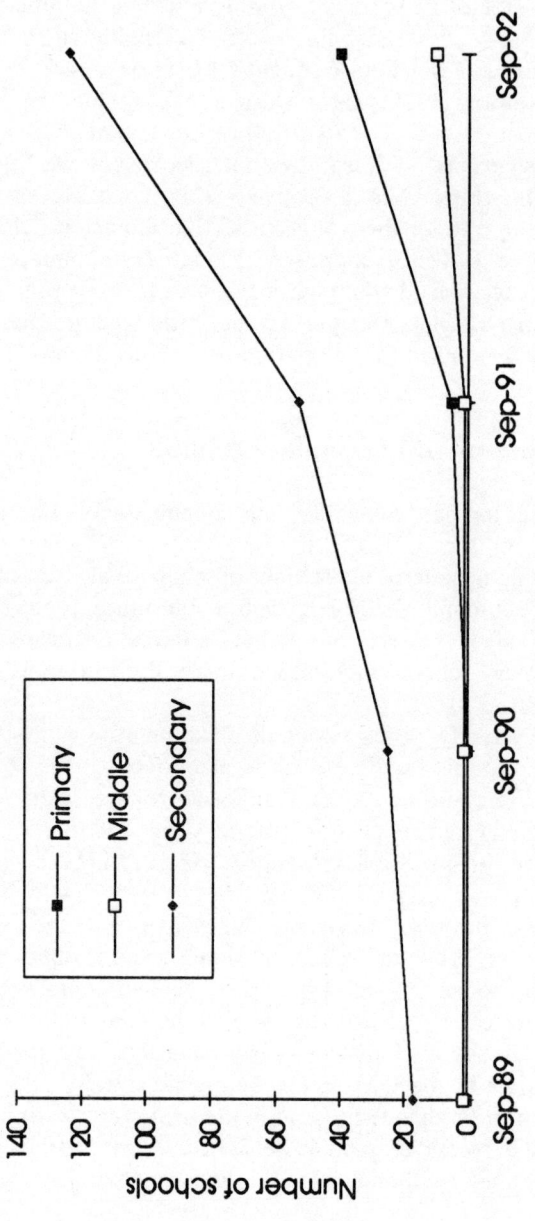

Figure 2.4 Types of schools which have achieved GM status

PATTERNS OF OPTING OUT

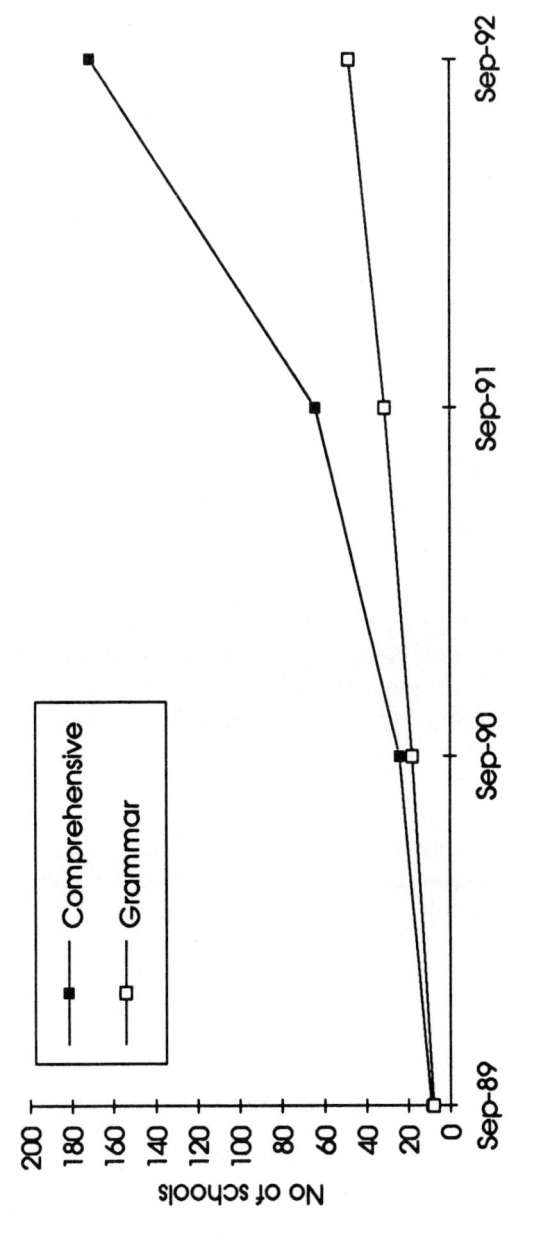

Figure 2.5 *Cumulative frequency of secondary schools achieving GM status by admissions policy*

rate of opting out increases, unless a significant number of GM schools change their admissions policies. After all, there are only 156 state-maintained grammar schools in England, and 40 per cent of these are already incorporated within the GM sector. For the time being, however, the relatively large number of selective GM schools is likely to be significant for both official comparisons and informal associations between sectors. With reference to the latter, it is noteworthy that many (we estimate approximately 46 per cent) of the comprehensive schools which have opted out are ex-grammar schools.

It should also be noted that there is a slightly higher representation of voluntary controlled and aided schools in the GM sector than in the LEA sector (nearly one-quarter as opposed to one-fifth). Although such schools are not necessarily academically selective, they are likely to have various forms of non-academic selection policy. The affinity between GM secondary schools and more traditional modes of education is further endorsed through the strong presence of single-sex and 11–18 schools. Although only 13 per cent of LEA schools prior to the GM schools policy offered single-sex provision, 29 per cent of GM secondary schools do. Similarly, while less than a half (44 per cent) of LEA schools have sixth forms, 75 per cent of GM secondary schools offer post-16 provision.

These figures, however, cannot be used without heavy qualification to support the thesis that opting out is leading to the extension of selective education 'by the back door'. But neither do they reflect well on some of the aspirations of the policy's early advocates, in particular those which stress the benefits of GM status for schools serving disadvantaged communities. Although such definitions are problematic, our questionnaire survey of LEAs shows that, out of 225 GM secondary schools, only 18 (ie, 8 per cent) serve what LEA officers consider to be areas of social disadvantage.

Summary

The scale, pace and distribution of opting out is characterized both by continuity and unevenness. In response to changes to the policy, there has been a steady growth in the GM sector. There are also recognizable trends in the motivations and types of schools which opt out. On the other hand, the distribution of GM schools is extremely patchy, with high concentrations in some areas and scarcity in others. It would be a mistake, however, to presume that the impact of opting out can be measured simply in terms of the density of GM schools. As we shall discuss in the next chapter, where we look at the effect of opting out on LEAs, the GM schools policy is likely to have profound consequences on the provision and organization of education, even in areas with numerically few GM schools.

Chapter 3
Local Education Authorities and Opting Out

This chapter examines the early impact of opting out on a selection of English LEAs. The analysis we offer is based on a series of in-depth interviews conducted with 24 LEA officers, each of whom, at the time of our fieldwork, was responsible for their local authority's policy on, and day-by-day response to, opting out. The interviews took place during late 1990 and early 1991. The LEAs involved comprised Conservative, Labour and Liberal Democrat-controlled authorities, and some where no political party had an overall majority.

Breaking the LEA monopoly

While it is rarely easy, and often inappropriate, to locate a straightforward ideological preference behind education policy, there can be little doubt that opting out is informed by a desire on the part of the government to move local authority functions in respect of education away from policy-making and related executive considerations towards mainly administrative and management priorities. Indeed, as we stressed in the Introduction and Chapter 1, this direction in government education policy is consistent with its approach to central-local relations in general and across a wide spectrum of welfare and service provision. The GM schools policy, therefore, needs to be seen as part of a broader strategic plan by the government to herald a new role for

LEAs in which they will be less occupied with maintaining a near monopoly of school provision and more concerned with greater overall efficiency linked to parental and user satisfaction within a diversified education market. Their functions thus redefined, LEAs will be expected to take increased responsibility, perhaps as agents of central government, for supervising, monitoring and reporting on standards in schools. Significantly, a version of this new role has been endorsed by the Audit Commission which refers to the LEA of the future as being, among other things, a 'provider of information to the education market, helping people to make informed choices' and a 'regulator of quality in schools and colleges' (Audit Commission, 1989). It resonates too with the prognoses of many academic commentators, not all of whom, significantly, could be regarded as supporters of the government's education policies (for example, Ranson, 1992).

Accordingly, the chief purpose behind our interviews with council officials was to explore how their authorities were responding to opting out, both generally, and in relation to particular schools. We were especially concerned to learn how far the existence of GM schools, or the strong possibility of schools wanting to opt out, was forcing LEAs to make adjustments to their strategic plans, particularly those concerned to rationalize surplus school places and reorganize secondary schools. We were also anxious to assess the impact of the policy on LEA finances, as well as to find out about any schemes to provide services to individual GM schools. Finally, we wanted to gauge how far the GM schools policy was leading to changes in the way in which LEAs relate to schools.

Period of consultation

As we mentioned in both the Introduction and Chapter 1, consultations about opting out were initiated in July 1987 following the publication by the government of a set of draft proposals (DES, 1987). While respondents other than LEAs made comments about their likely impact, we intend, given the focus of this chapter, to concentrate on those from local authority sources.

To no one's great surprise, most local authorities did not welcome the idea of opted-out schools. LEAs were either opposed in principle to the policy, or concerned about its practical consequences, which they judged mostly negatively. In the event, the government noted, but ignored, their warnings, no doubt thinking that few LEAs would be likely to support proposals that could result in schools leaving their control. While that may be so, the more significant feature of the government's attitude was that it signalled a further confirmation that the 'partnership' said to exist between central and local government was undergoing redefinition and transformation.

LEA reaction to the draft proposals was centred on two broad concerns which addressed, in turn, the likely impact of opting out on the distribution, rationalization and planning of local school provision and its potentially damaging consequences for the financing of education.

Most LEAs were adamant that the opportunity to opt out would have the undesirable effect of either inhibiting or frustrating their capacity to develop sensible plans for the rationalization of surplus school places. They argued that a school threatened with closure, amalgamation or reorganization would try to become GM and thus undermine the LEA's capacity to plan strategically. The Association of Metropolitan Authorities was particularly anxious about this predicted effect of the policy:

> LEAs are still under an obligation to remove surplus school places, but unless the Secretary of State makes it clear that he would not view sympathetically applications for grant-maintained status which appear to arise largely from a school's desire to avoid the consequences of reorganization, rationalization schemes will be inhibited. (AMA, 1988).

Equally concerned was the Society of Education Officers:

> The proposals will delay rationalization of provision ... LEAs may well feel discouraged from embarking on consideration of rationalization plans (SEO, 1988).

If such plans were not discouraged, the policy, it was felt, could have the equally undesirable consequence of leading some LEAs to propose closing schools that they would otherwise wish to keep open. Indeed, where this was part of a larger plan designed to respond to falling rolls, there was also the danger that surplus school capacity would simply be shuffled around rather than tackled strategically.

Associated with these concerns was another which linked overall planning capacity with parental choice. Because a local authority has little influence on, or awareness of, how parents exercise choice between its schools and those which opt out, it was feared that this would make it difficult for LEAs to plan for, or predict, the scale of provision they should be making overall. Commenting on this anxiety, the Audit Commission (1988) drew attention to its likely financial implications:

> If it (the LEA) wishes to be sure to have enough places for all pupils who need them, it will have to maintain a large surplus of capacity in its own schools. This would be extremely expensive.

Expensive or not, LEAs remained unconvinced that the policy would promote greater parental choice. In this connection, one of the government's fiercest critics was, again, the Association of Metropolitan Authorities:

> The argument that permitting schools to opt out for grant-maintained status will promote diversity and choice seems to us to be mere casuistry. The choice will be exercised by a particular group of parents at a particular time and will bind future generations of parents and children to a given form of education and type of school (AMA, 1988).

Bracketed with this concern was a set of others, all of which stressed the alleged unfairness of the policy and its potentially unsettling effects and divisive consequences. The policy, it was argued, would fragment and disrupt the education service by preventing LEAs from providing a public service organized on a planned, coherent and equitable basis. The London Borough of Brent, for example, was extremely pessimistic in its assessment of the policy's impact on local authorities:

> The ability of an LEA to set up administrative systems according to principles of fairness, reasonableness and the best interests of all schools and all pupils over such crucially important matters as admissions ... and central services ... will become impossible.... This could result in an invidiously divisive system ... of schools throughout the country. LEAs could have little more than a residuary function providing education largely for those children who could not gain admission to, or who were excluded from, the other kinds of schools (Brent LEA, 1988).

Similarly, the Association of County Councils warned that:

The consequences for the education of the great majority who would not be in grant-maintained schools could vary widely. Services which have built up over many years to benefit areas... would be inevitably disrupted and weakened. An element of seemingly permanent instability would be injected into the provision of public education (ACC, 1988).

Finally, and complementing the earlier concerns of the Audit Commission, disquiet was expressed about the implications of the policy for local educational finance in general. Tim Brighouse, formerly Chief Education Officer in Oxfordshire, for example, stated that for local authorities to survive they would have to

avoid the diseconomies of too many schools opting out, because each one that does increases the burden of central overheads for others and therefore an LEA's own stability ... (Brighouse, 1989).

Barnet's Director of Education was equally despondent:

The more schools opt out, the more serious the problem will become. With each school that leaves the authority, unit costs rise and eventually a critical point is reached where it no longer makes financial sense to have an authority (Gill, 1989).

The Society of Education Officers, while less extravagant in its predictions, was unhappy none the less with what it thought would be an awkward period of adjustment for LEAs:

The proposals would involve inefficient and ineffective use of available funds and lead to wasteful duplication and loss of economies of scale, together with additional costs for LEAs ... without any benefit to the service. They would make the planning of a coherent, sensible, overall system of education in an area much more difficult (SEO, 1988).

LEAs' experience of opted-out schools

But how far does the actual experience of LEAs affected by schools opting out match the dire predictions made on their behalf about the policy before it took effect? We suspect that the answer to this question is less unequivocal than many of the policy's critics would care to admit, though in Chapter 7 we conclude, in the light of more recent events, that LEAs have a very uncertain, if not bleak, future ahead of them.

As to what reliance can be placed on the conclusions reached on the basis of our research, the key variable must be the proportion of schools in a single authority which had been approved for GM status at the time of our interviews. Few of the LEAs we visited were having to adjust to more than three schools leaving their control. To that extent, it could be argued that, for most of these LEAs, the policy was of little consequence. That conclusion, however, is not one the LEAs concerned would be happy for us to report here, not least because they could foresee more of their schools opting out as time went on. Indeed, three of the LEAs in our original sample have 'lost' in excess of 30 per cent of their secondary schools in the last 18 months. Thus, while we report the perceptions of LEA officers at a relatively early stage in the policy's implementation, some trends were apparent in the first months of 1990 and remain significant to the present day.

LEA strategic planning and opting out

All of the LEAs we visited were introducing measures to remove surplus school places. In some of them, as one would expect, these measures usually formed part of a broader development including the introduction of new forms of provision such as non-selective schooling, co-education and sixth-form colleges. In every case, such plans entailed the closure or redesignation of existing schools. In many, there was reported a direct link between a perceived or actual threat of closure and/or redesignation and a school seeking to opt out, a fact which underlines some of the statistics discussed in Chapter 2.

It is not our intention to comment upon the merits of any reorganization plan. In any event, that was not an issue about which we sought clarification during our visits to local authorities. Clearly, though, one of the central issues at stake for both an LEA and the Secretary of State in the debate about the appropriateness of a school becoming GM is whether or not it is 'viable'. No doubt many schools threatened with closure by their LEAs are viable in terms of pupil numbers. But viewed from the perspective of the LEA, the viability of a local system of provision made up of a number of schools may require the closure or amalgamation of some institutions which have adequate pupil numbers but whose continuation would have negative financial or educational consequences for the rest. In other words, there may arise occasions when the Secretary of State, in the course of considering an opting-out proposal, would not share an LEA's interpretation of an individual school's viability. Such conflicts of interest between the Secretary of State and LEAs are likely given that the DfE considers a school's application for GM status before any local authority reorganization plan which may have a bearing on its future.

It became very clear to us in the course of our visits to LEAs that many of their reorganization plans had either been abandoned or temporarily shelved in the wake of schools seeking or having achieved GM status. This outcome was reported by almost two-thirds of the LEA officers we interviewed. The following edited extracts from our interviews illustrate the nature and strength of LEA frustration with this consequence of the policy. They also highlight the manner in which it has forced some of them to seek alternative courses of action and inhibited others:

> It has put a complete brake on reviews right across the county in all sorts of respects ... (Conservative-controlled council).
> The policy has caused us to stop and think about secondary reorganization.... It has slowed the process down considerably.... What we are doing is almost starting again ... (No overall control).
> The GM proposal not only put into limbo the provision for one area, it also has taken apart the sensible provision for a wider area as well... (Conservative-controlled).
> When the school got its go-ahead to become grant-maintained ... the plans we had for it had to be abandoned.... When we came back to Committee ... we had to say ... we think you must only put forward proposals that will not provoke opposition from any quarter ... (Liberal Democrat-controlled).

However, seven LEAs were unable to report either any disruption to their existing planning for school places because of the existence of GM schools or any feelings of being intimidated by the policy:

> Grant-maintained schools are an integral part of the provision in certain areas of this county.... We have not withdrawn any proposals for reorganization as a consequence of grant-maintained schools (Conservative-controlled).

> The policy has not compromised the LEA's willingness to go forward with rationalization plans. We are pressing ahead and we shall take it one step at a time.... In any event, I do not believe the Secretary of State is going to help schools to become grant-maintained where an LEA is wanting to make a better and sensible use of its existing resources.... We are not threatened by this policy. We will try to do things in such a way that our schools will not want to opt out (No overall control).

On the other hand, several LEAs felt that, while the GM schools policy was not entirely frustrating their planning functions, it was making it more difficult to operationalize them. Typical of this reaction was the following comment:

> It was always difficult for the LEA to close schools, though we managed it. GMS makes it more difficult. For, however sound a closure plan might be, it can now be overturned by the preferences of a minority ... (Conservative-controlled).

How far observations of this kind indicate that some LEAs exaggerate the negative impact of opting out by overestimating the difference it makes to their ability to remove spare capacity is difficult for us to gauge. Certainly, it makes some difference; but there may be a sense in which some LEAs, in expressing opposition to the policy, make too much of their earlier powers which they contrast positively with those they have presently. As Wallace (1990) observes:

> ... previous local powers (to provide the right number of pupil places in the right places) were not as great or as effective as sometimes supposed. The possibility of change sometimes makes the past and the present seem more attractive than they are (p 228).

Ranson's study (1990) of the impact of contraction on three local authorities reinforces this point insofar as it highlights the extent to which, and in advance of the GM schools policy, delay and inconsistency at the centre either caused or compounded inertia in particular localities. For the fact remains that closing schools has always been a long drawn out affair, and particularly so since the passage of the 1980 Education Act which strengthens the powers of the Education Secretary to regulate the balance of planning and choice between LEAs and parents. Even so, the number of surplus places approved by the

Secretary of State to be removed by LEAs has dropped significantly in the last two years. In 1990, over 145,000 places were removed; in 1991, less than 80,000. How far this reduction was influenced by the GM schools policy is impossible to determine, though one can reasonably speculate that opting out may have intimidated some LEAs into not drawing up reorganization plans to remove surplus places which involve closing schools.

In this connection, it is important to emphasize that a single opted-out school can have a significant impact on an LEA's capacity to plan effectively if it occupies a particularly pivotal position within its anticipated scheme of provision. During our visits to LEAs we learned of several instances where, after lengthy consultations involving every conceivable vested interest group, a school faced by closure or a change of character had sought and achieved GM status and, as a result, sabotaged local plans to develop, in one case, a tertiary college, in another, non-selective co-education. For both the LEAs concerned, there appeared to be little further room for manoeuvre except, that is, for them to identify another school to close which it was then feared would also seek to opt out:

> It's going to make the LEA anxious about going forward with other rationalization plans. There is a fear that if we designated another area for reorganization ... that it would lead to a further application for grant-maintained status. There is a feeling that, if one school has achieved it in the authority, then others may be willing to try as well ... (No overall control).
>
> The policy has injected a very significant doubt in the minds of our local politicians that if they proposed any sort of scheme that seems to disadvantage 11–18 schools they would immediately have another opt out campaign on their hands ... (Labour-controlled).

LEA relations with schools that opt out

Not unexpectedly, it was some of the Labour-controlled LEAs of those we visited which, for the time being, had determined to have only minimal contact with those of its schools which had opted out. Their attitudes are summed up as follows:

> The LEA will only provide those services which it is required to by law, but no others.... The attitude of the elected members is that the

school voted to opt out and to cease to be part of the LEA.... It cannot then turn round and pick and choose which bits they want to come back into.... It has made its bed and it must lie on it... (Labour-controlled).

Once the school had decided to go GM, the Council took the view that the authority would provide only those services it was obliged to provide.... If the school really felt strongly enough to want to sever its links with the LEA, the Council was not then going to try to restore these links in a different way. So we honour our statutory obligations, but do nothing else ... (Labour-controlled)

On the other hand, another official, also from a Labour-controlled authority, regretted the negative attitude of his elected members:

As Acting Director of Education, I have continually requested members to maintain close relations pointing out that the children in question remain pupils under the patronage of this LEA and that they may well come back to our schools at a later stage ... (Labour-controlled).

In fact, this view was the one that we more often heard. Thus, despite the high degree of antipathy to the policy felt by many of the LEAs within which we interviewed, fuelled occasionally by alleged misrepresentations of their motives by supporters of opting out, the majority were anxious to develop positive relations with 'their' GM schools. Moreover, such relations were being fostered regardless of the political colour of the LEAs concerned. As the following extracts illustrate, their reasons for doing so are partly financial and partly educational:

We have always said, and it is one of the principles we have tried to work on, that the children who attend the grant-maintained school are still our children. They are still part of the maintained sector; that hasn't changed because the school has become grant-maintained. We have a duty to those children. The school is still part of our local provision.... It has also been our policy stance from the start to continue to provide at cost any service the school wants ... (No overall control).

In our initial policy statement it was agreed that the LEA would have dealings with schools that opted out.... Our view was that schools which achieve grant-maintained status will be here to stay. It is not sensible therefore to adopt a negative policy ... (Conservative-controlled).

We will enter into working relations with schools that opt out. Indeed we have already done so.... Also we took the initiative in offering them services.... One school in fact has bought into a number of services including payroll and cleaning and maintenance.... It has also bought into our inspection and advisory service.... It is rather important for us as an authority to continue to provide such services at these schools because the less we do for them the less cost-effective becomes our whole operation (Conservative-controlled).

Significantly, a Chief Education Officer, whose borough was once strongly identified with municipal socialism, was equally concerned to foster a working accommodation with the local GM school:

I am empowered by the Education Committee to seek to develop a fruitful relationship and to seek to contract delivery of some services. So far we haven't yet set out in detail what all these services will be, but we hope to do so very soon.... Certainly we hope to provide some INSET. We are also going to tender to provide catering.... I am pleased to say that the head of the GM school still attends our heads' meetings and the Director's monthly briefing.... That hasn't changed ... (Labour-controlled).

Across the political spectrum, LEAs appear to be heeding the advice of the Audit Commission (1989) which recommends that local authorities should 'cooperate' with schools that opt out of their control. Certainly, many of the LEAs within which we did our research have given an undertaken to provide information to parents about GM schools, though the amount of detail varies from place to place. Others have also agreed financial packages for the community use of existing sports and leisure facilities located on the sites of GM schools, while a few have offered them 'associate membership'.

LEA finance and opted-out schools

It is clear, then, that most LEAs adopt a pragmatic as opposed to political response to the GM schools policy. That is to say, while they mostly do not like or welcome the policy, they regard it as more expedient to work with, rather than against, its grain. High among the factors which they take into account in developing this attitude are considerations of finance, an area of potential destabilization that, it will be recalled, opponents of opting out were quick to highlight during the consultation period about the policy.

In our investigation we found little evidence to support the view that the current number of GM schools is creating great financial difficulties for all the LEAs affected, though a number of the officers we spoke to were concerned about a future in which a substantial number of their schools had opted out, while several others also complained about what they considered to be over-generous capital grant allocations. The following extracts, each derived from a different LEA source, are typical of much of our data on this aspect of the policy's effects:

> In practical terms, when you have over 700 schools, the loss of one, or even two, doesn't have a devastating effect. Financially, they take with them a share of the central costs of the authority ... but in this case we have simply stood the loss.... As for the capital allocations, I think there is a lot of truth in the suggestion that they have got more by opting out than they would have got if they had stayed with the local authority. We did a calculation which suggests that each grant-maintained school has got, on average, ten times what we have through our capital allocation for our individual schools ... (Labour-controlled).
>
> The one GM school hasn't had much effect financially on the LEA.... It's a very small school after all.... If we started to lose larger schools ... then we could get into difficulty ... (Conservative-controlled).
>
> The significance of this development will depend on the number of schools as a proportion of the total that are given grant-maintained status. I think we could possibly deal with, say, 25 per cent of schools in this LEA becoming grant-maintained.... I think if there were more we might be destabilized.... We can cope, then, up to a point. But there would come a time when it would be literally a financial and managerial loss to the LEA as a result of which we simply would not be able to do certain things which are required by law (Conservative-controlled).

While most of the LEA officers we interviewed conceded that their authorities were not under a great financial burden as a result of a few of their schools opting out, we anticipate that their views on this matter will undergo change as the full implications of the financial measures outlined in the 1993 Education Act are realized. Indeed, we say more about this in our extended discussion of the Act's implications in the final chapter of this book.

Summary and conclusion

Our interviews within LEAs affected by opted-out schools permit us to draw three conclusions. First, many local authorities find it deeply frustrating that their planning functions can be so easily prejudiced by schools wanting to opt out. Second, despite this outcome, and for a mixture of educational and pragmatic reasons, most of them prefer to develop working relations with those of its schools which become GM. Third, there is no evidence currently to hand which indicates that great financial difficulties arise when one or two secondary schools opt out from the same local authority. Having said that, many LEAs anticipated a time when an enlarged GM schools sector will begin seriously to deplete their financial resources, so making it difficult for them to meet their obligations to schools remaining within their control.

Despite the attack made on their role by the GM schools policy, many LEAs appear to be resigned to the fact that they will need to make significant adjustments to their philosophy and working practices in light of an increase in the number of schools opting out. As one officer, interestingly from a Labour-controlled authority, said to us:

> I think there continues to be a very important role for us to carry out.... If we are going to exert an influence – which seems to me to be the essence of our future role – we must develop good relations with all the people and institutions we want to influence, and that includes GM schools. Even if they're not playing on our pitch, we can't afford to keep the ball out (Labour-controlled).

How far LEAs with much reduced powers and budgets can realistically expect to influence schools which are no longer within their direct orbit of responsibility is one of the issues we take up in our final chapter. In the meantime, and in any event, it is clear that one group of people with which LEAs will increasingly be concerned to develop 'good relations' is headteachers of GM schools, and it is to their experience of the opting-out process that we turn in the next chapter.

Chapter 4
Headteachers and Opting Out

In this chapter we examine the process of opting out through the eyes of 19 headteachers of established GM schools, all of whom agreed to be interviewed as part of our larger study of the policy's impact. As in other chapters, we begin this one with a résumé of the reasoning behind this aspect of our research and some details about the headteachers whom we interviewed.

The purpose of the headteacher interviews was to learn something about the background to schools seeking GM status, including the role which heads play in the process. We were concerned to learn too what advantages headteachers felt accrued from their schools having opted out. We also wanted to gauge the impact of the policy on their work, including relations with parents, governors and other members of staff.

As Table 4.1 indicates, our interviewees make up an appropriate representative sample inasmuch as they include headteachers of all the different kinds of secondary school found in the GM sector at the beginning of the academic year 1990/91.

Our research, which began one year earlier, coincided with the opening of the first group of 14 secondary schools approved as GM establishments. The headteachers of eight of the institutions which make up this initial wave of GM schools took part in our research. They were interviewed in all cases at least three terms after their schools were incorporated as GM institutions. The rest of the sample includes

Table 4.1 *Headteacher interviews*

Type of GM school	Operating at 1.9.90	Headteacher interviews
Comprehensive (mixed)	17 (39%)	7 (37%)
Comprehensive (single-sex)	8 (18%) 57%	4 (21%) 58%
Grammar (mixed)	6 (13%)	3 (16%)
Grammar (single-sex)	13 (30%) 43%	5 (26%) 42%
Totals:	44 (100%)	19 (100%)

11 headteachers whose schools became GM in the second year of the policy's implementation.

While the headteachers we interviewed reflect accurately the sort of establishments which first achieved GM status, they clearly are not representative of the GM sector as it is now. At the time of the interviews, there were no headteachers of GM primary schools; today there are over 60. More critically, the actual number of schools that make up the sector has grown eightfold in size since we conducted the interviews. Despite these changes in the size and composition of the GM sector, the accounts obtained from our sample of headteachers have a special salience. For it is the widely and flatteringly reported experiences of many of them (see, for instance, Chubb and Moe, 1992a, 1992b) which have given the policy its public face and, in turn, legitimated a particular view of its merits.

It is also important to stress that some of the schools which feature strongly in government promotional literature about GM status (see DES, 1991, for example) are not only ones within which we interviewed, but also institutions whose headteachers have been in the vanguard of those assisting the policy's development. Three of our respondents, for example, are founder members of the Standing Advisory Committee (Headteachers) for Grant Maintained Schools (SAC) which is 'the formal channel of communication for GM schools, the Department for Education and Ministers' (GM Schools Centre, 1992b). These headteachers therefore act as informal spokespersons for the GM sector. Thus, while we do not want to elevate any of them to the status of policy-maker, we do want to say many are significant government 'sounding boards' who help to shape the conditions within which policy decisions are ultimately made. Thus interpreted, their perceptions and accounts are especially important. Moreover, potential incomers to the GM schools sector frequently seek the advice of some of our headteachers before proceeding with their own bids to opt out. Accordingly, many of the headteachers we interviewed face two ways: they look up to and cooperate with ministers, and down at and assist prospective recruits to the GM sector. In this way they help to produce and reproduce the policy.

Factors influencing a move towards GM status

As we indicated in both Chapters 2 and 3, the reasons which lead schools to seek GM status are not always straightforward. Having said that, one of the more ironic aspects of opting out is the extent to which it is pursued initially for negative rather than positive reasons. That is to say, in the early stages of the process of seeking GM status, 'becoming grant-maintained' is frequently interpreted as a way of avoiding something considered threatening, such as an LEA proposal to close or reorganize a school, rather than a means of embracing something new, such as providing an opportunity to manage a school in a different and innovative way. Many of the accounts offered by our sample of 19 GM headteachers bear out this point (see Table 4.2). Seven of their schools were subject to a Section 12 or 13 proposal. Accordingly, their wish to become GM was prompted by an uncomplicated desire to survive and stay open. Moreover, the remaining 12 schools also include four institutions that wanted to thwart an LEA reorganization plan under early discussion and two others who sought to forestall one emerging. In other words, in these cases, the mere discussion of possible closure or change of character had been enough to trigger the GM process:

> The school had been the subject of several previous reorganization schemes, none of which had come to anything. Although we were not, at the time of the ballot, part of a new reorganization plan, least of all a Section 12 or 13 proposal, we felt threatened ... and so we thought of opting out ... (Headteacher T).

Table 4.2 *Chief reason cited for schools seeking GM status*

To challenge an existing Section 12 or 13 proposal	7
To frustrate discussion of a reorganization plan	6
To obtain additional income	4
To manage their affairs independently of the LEA	2

The individualist emphasis of opting out

In four cases (see Table 4.2), each involving a school the future of which was assured, the wish to opt out was prompted instead by the feeling that the LEA was providing insufficient resources and that GM status would be financially advantageous. The following comment of one of the headteachers concerned could have been made by any of them:

> I looked at the (Education Reform) Act and saw the possibilities GM status offered. I looked at what we had and what we could get.... From where else could we have got a grant for a quarter of a million? ... We have been pushing the LEA for years for that kind of money to improve this school ... (Headteacher H).

In considering his own school's financial needs in this way, this headteacher, like others we interviewed, is drawn unwittingly into offering tacit support to that aspect of opting out which is designed to 'reorientate producers from a service ethic towards a sense of competitive self-interest' (Ball, 1992b). Indeed, having helped to take their schools out of LEA control, headteachers' sense of being part of a larger public service appears to undergo a major shift in emphasis. What chiefly concerns most of them is to obtain the best possible deal for their own institutions irrespective of its consequences for the effective administration of the local education services they leave behind. This attitude contrasts very much with that found in a recent report of the perceptions of 32 headteachers from eight LEAs whose schools had resolved not to consider opting out. Specifically, Brown and Baker (1992) reveal that most of the heads in their sample think that GM status runs against the 'spirit of cooperation', and that their LEAs are doing the best they can given the financial limitations and other constraints within which they have to operate.

GM school heads, on the other hand, are not so sympathetic to the plight of their former LEAs. At the 1992 GM Schools Annual Conference, for example, most of the headteachers present warmly applauded a speech by the former DES Minister of State, Tim Eggar, in which he launched an extravagent attack on the policies, motives and expenditure priorities of LEAs. Of course, such attacks are not particular either to government ministers or headteachers of GM schools. A lot of heads who run LEA-maintained schools presumably draw periodic attention to their employers' alleged incompetence and parsimony. But what we detect is something qualitatively different in the comments of some of the GM headteachers we interviewed which amounts to a greater capacity, not only to use the rhetoric of looking chiefly to one's own institutional needs, but to make a virtue of this position. Consider the following extract:

> The capital formula allocation used to go straight into the LEA's coffers, and they would probably have said somebody else's need is greater than ours. Maybe they're right. But it is, after all, only a relatively small amount of money which I have been able to do a lot with ... (Headteacher N).

This extract illustrates neatly a contradiction that many GM headteachers struggle with, but which the GM policy helps them to sidestep. On the one hand, the respondent is able to acknowledge that other schools might have needs greater than his own; but, on the other hand, the policy of opting out provides a cover for him to appear to be sanguine about depriving them of resources in order to make use of them in his own institution.

The role of the head in seeking GM status

Whatever the initial motivation to become GM, a significant number of the headteachers we interviewed took the main part initially in pursuing the possibility of opting out (see Table 4.3). Although large numbers of parents participate enthusiastically in ballots to determine whether schools can make applications to the Secretary of State to opt out, it appears their role in the process is largely a passive one by comparison with that played by headteachers. Moreover, Rogers (1992) goes further, claiming that parents are often used as mere 'ballot fodder'. We have some evidence to confirm this. Our data suggest that heads are often very much to the fore in *initial* discussions about GM status. If we exclude the three headteachers in our sample who took up their posts

Table 4.3 *Prime-movers in the opting out process (N=19)*

Headteachers in association with the chair of governors	9
Parent action groups	3
Groups of governors with only the tacit support of the head	7

either shortly before or immediately after their schools became GM, the greater number of the rest (9/16) acted as prime-movers in the opting-out process. That is to say, they first sought out information about the policy, subsequently persuaded governors of the merits of GM status, and then lobbied resolutely for a 'Yes' vote during the run-up to the parental ballot. The following comments are typical of the ones we derived from these headteachers, all of whom declared their support for the policy at a very early stage:

> I played a key role.... I felt very definitely that GM status would provide the opportunity to continue doing what we wanted to do as a grammar school, and the chair of governors felt the same. So, it would be fair to say that we spearheaded the attack. We conducted the public meetings and we did most of the public speaking (Headteacher M).
>
> It all began with a report from me to the governors in which I summarized the main provisions of the Reform Act including GM status.... I laid before them what I felt were the advantages and disdavantages of opting out.... They saw that I had very positive feelings towards it ... that it was a road I was prepared to tread and take responsibility for (Headteacher L).

Parents and the process of opting out

Parent action groups taking the chief responsibility for initiating the opting-out process were in evidence in only three of the schools where we conducted interviews. On the other hand, groups of governors, frequently working alongside headteachers, a few of whom were agnostic about the merits of opting out, were significant catalytic agents. Their role in this connection was mentioned by seven of the headteachers we interviewed, as, for example, in the following typical extract:

> The prime movers, initially, were one or two governors.... I sat on the fence and it was damned painful.... I strove to be neutral and accurate ... (Headteacher Q).

The 'fence-sitters' excepted, the chief impression gained is that many headteachers are very happy to play a leading role in pursuing the GM option on behalf of their schools. Moreover, among this group are a few who do not, in any event, view the GM schools policy as being one that should concern parents to any great degree. On the contrary, the policy, as they see it, is about 'better' management, not enhanced opportunities for parental involvement, least of all greater parental control:

> GM is a management tool. As far as parents are concerned, it doesn't and shouldn't affect them ... (Headteacher A).
> GM is really about management and finance and, as far as possible, I would rather parents were not troubled too much by either ... (Headteacher Q).

These last observations complement other data obtained from interviews we conducted with over one hundred parents whose children attend GM schools managed by eight of the headteachers included in our sample, the perceptions of whom are subjected to more thoroughgoing analysis in parts of both Chapters 5 and 6. While we report there that the overwhelming majority of these parents speak favourably of their children's schools, often claiming they are the 'best around', we stress too that less than one-third (ie, 29 per cent) say they have a greater sense of control since they opted out. In fact, only a minority (35 per cent) claim they are familiar with the names and identities of *any* of the governors of their children's schools.

Headteachers, governors and opting out

Governors of GM schools occupy an ambiguous position as managers. While their legal and formal duties are clearly spelled out both in law and government regulation, their managerial responsibilities, vis-à-vis the headteacher, are less explicitly formulated. Though Deem and Wilkins (1992) report excellent working relations in one GM school, our data offer hints that some headteachers are struggling to come to grips with the new form of governor accountability which their schools' change in status had brought about. For example:

> I think there is a distinction between governing and managing, and managing is a pretty difficult job.... Within the committees of the governing body things began to be polarized. I felt that they were trying to do my job ... (Headteacher A).
>
> Certain decisions are clearly the responsibility of the whole governing body. It can't delegate decisions relating to either the curriculum or finance. But in practice that can be ponderous, and we've got to find a way of getting over it ... (Headteacher N).

'To find a way of getting over it' might be interpreted as the need to look for ways in which the essential tasks of school management can be facilitated without undue governor involvement. Although there is no suggestion that this should entail a diminishment in headteacher accountability, there is an intimation that the role of governors in school decision-making should be clarified and ultimately restrieved. To that extent, and conjoined with the ambivalence shown towards greater parental involvement reflected in earlier extracts, what we have here are indications that, at the point of implementation, the GM schools policy does not carry with it any overriding commitment to either greater openness or new forms of democratic control of education. We go further to suggest that, rather than provide a new parents' or governors' charter, GM status encourages a novel kind of 'producer interest' in the form of headteacher control which this government appears pleased to endorse, possibly because, as we shall argue later, it helps to implement the policy and other associated educational reforms.

The head's sense of representing a new form of 'producer interest', however, is likely to be experienced differently by the teaching staff of different GM schools. Much depends on the extent to which teachers feel they are implicated in policy-making decisions and the concerns of management. But, as with the involvement of parents and governors, nothing necessarily follows for teachers' sense of professional empowerment once GM status is achieved. If anything, as Thompson's (1992) survey of the experience of 'going grant-maintained' indicates, the existing management style of headteachers is as likely to be consolidated as radically altered once their schools have opted out. Thus headteachers who previously eschewed delegation, and who ordinarily prefer to make important decisions without consultation, are unlikely to feel compelled to operate in more collegial ways once their schools become GM. In fact, GM status may strengthen rather than dilute their existing executive control. As one of our respondents put it:

> My power has considerably increased and improved. I say 'improved'; my colleagues might say 'worsened'! ... (Headteacher A).

Either way, running a GM school can result in an increase in the distance of some headteachers from the mainstream concerns of classroom teachers. This form of isolation, which is partly reflected also in the early reported experience of headteachers of LEA-LMS schools (see Arnott *et al.*, 1992, for example), is very evident in our data. Some respondents, for example, find the burden of their managerial and administrative work so great that they feel compelled to give up classroom teaching:

> My job has changed enormously.... I'm not teaching this year for the first time.... I'm glad I made that decision, though. Something would have suffered if I hadn't, either the quality of my teaching or something else ... (Headteacher G).

The decision of some headteachers to remove themselves from the timetable, of course, carries with it the risk that they may become cut off from the very activity with which most staff are routinely concerned and partly in terms of which their legitimacy as the school's 'leading professional' is measured. It also increases the likelihood of creating in schools a sharper division of labour than has existed hitherto between those who chiefly manage (ie, engage mainly in handling personnel matters, financial planning, income generation and marketing) and those who mostly teach. Ball (1992a) argues that this new and tighter form of boundary maintenance assists headteachers to regulate better and scrutinize further the working practices of teacher subordinates. He also thinks that it helps generally to obscure potential conflicts between the drive for 'productivity' and the needs of pupils as identified by their teachers, thus constituting 'the basis for a classic polarization between the values of professional responsibility and those of efficient management' (1992b). While our respondents never explicitly acknowledge this distinction, their observations about the changing nature of their work seem to imply it:

> The pattern of my working life has changed. It is proving to be quite a problem because of the number of meetings I now have to

attend.... I'm far more concerned with financial aspects which have brought me for the first time into the realm of negotiating contracts.... I'm also more involved in personnel work and employee relations such as grievance procedures.... That's all very different from the work I did before ... (Headteacher G).

I might describe this place as a 'state school', but it's more like a limited company. I have a 'board of directors' and I am a kind of 'managing director'. I am now less concerned with specific problems and much more involved with financial and personnel management... (Headteacher C).

The 'regulated autonomy' of GM schools

But there is a further related aspect to consider which focuses on the relationship which GM schools and their headteachers have with the government and its education policies. Unlike LEA-maintained schools, GM establishments are directly linked to a department of state, the DfE. Thus, in contrast to their counterparts employed in the LEA sector, GM school heads are positioned in such a way that they mediate government policy more or less undiluted:

I am the only professional adviser to the governors on educational matters. Previously, a document would come from the LEA saying we ought to be doing this or that. Now the documentation comes direct to me and I have to make sure we implement it. When I was with the LEA it was very easy to be lazy, though I never was. But some lazy heads were dragged along because the LEA was always there to pick up the pieces and offer security.... There's no more of that. You're on your own ... (Headteacher G).

In effect, the headteachers of GM schools can be said to be personal conduits for the literal receipt and 'delivery' of government education policy, rather than persons who act in concert, say, with a supportive LEA and/or colleagues in neighbouring schools, to protect staff, pupils and parents from its alleged worst excesses. As one GM headteacher observed:

My job used to include overseeing the curriculum. Now that function has been taken away from me by the National Curriculum legislation. I'm not overseeing so much as managing an imposed curriculum. That still requires a tremendous amount of work, but it doesn't require an excecutive function. It's much more managerial and clerical. At the end of the day, all I am doing is making sure the requirements are being met ... (Headteacher C).

While GM school headteachers undoubtedly experience a different sense of freedom as a consequence of running 'self-governing' institutions, it is a freedom to deploy additional income largely to expedite the smooth implementation of government policy. Without being conscious of the process, GM school headteachers are thus progressively coopted by central government and their establishments turned into 'state' schools in a quite genuine sense. The 'trick' played on GM headteachers entails the proposition that educational reform is being done *by* their schools, when in reality it is mostly being done *to* them (Ball, 1992c).

The rhetoric of institutional autonomy plays a crucial role in creating the impression that GM status confers greater independence on state schools than that enjoyed by establishments that operate under the control of a local authority. In reality, as we stress thoughout this book, the autonomy of GM schools (as of LEA establishments, for that matter) is enormously constrained. Self-governing status does not extend to either kind of school decisions about their ultimate goals, who they can admit, what they can teach, and how they want to be governed. This 'regulated autonomy' (Dale, 1989) conveniently helps the government to 'steer' state schools 'at a distance' (Kickert, 1991), and in directions of its choosing. These 'directions' include not only mainstream policies such as those affecting the National Curriculum, pupil assessment and teacher appraisal, but also 'pet' initiatives like the enhancement of technological education in schools, for which the GM sector is in receipt of special extra funding, and the diversification of school provision through DfE approval of the right of GM comprehensive schools to select either on aptitude or ability a minority of their pupils. 'Steering at a distance' has the additional advantage for the government of enabling it to avoid responsibility for anything that goes wrong as these policies are implemented, while taking most of the credit when they 'succeed'.

The advantages of opting out

The headteachers of GM schools, however, do not appear to have any great sense of being central to the government's broad strategy for reformimg education. If they do have such feelings, they are mostly obscured by the realization that opting out has secured for them considerable financial advantage. Certainly this is the benefit of opting out to which all them give chief priority (see Table 4.4). The following extract is typical of the sort of claims made on behalf of opting out by our respondents:

> There are a great many benefits. For a start we have more money as well as the freedom to actually spend it in the way we see fit.... You can get on with things. Decisions about maintenance can be instant. I don't have to wait for the roof to fall in ... (Headteacher K).

With additional funding come more staff, better pay, improved levels of resourcing and higher standards of decor:

> ... the total teaching staff has risen by three full-time equivalents.... We have twice as many modern language assistants; twice as much peripatetic music.... We have introduced a teacher support service.... We have increased the number of responsibility allowances by a third.... We have introduced bonus payments.... At least 50 per cent of the staff are financially quite considerably better off.... We spend twice as much on books and equipment than we used to.... If you look around, you'll find areas of the school that have got paint on them for the first time in years. If you ... talk to staff, they'll say they are better paid, work in a much more attractive environment and that their jobs are easier ... (Headteacher C).

Table 4.4 *Advantages of opting out*

Named advantage	No. of mentions
Additional income	19
Increased freedom to deploy income	19
Increased capacity to make decisions	5
Independence from LEA control/policies	3
Increased job satisfaction	2
Greater sense of mission	1

Opting for a 'traditional' education?

The implications of extra income, however, are never discussed in ways that articulate with innovative projects to increase educational opportunity and improve levels of pupil achievement, though both are assumed to follow automatically from the preferential financial treatment associated with GM status. Thus, while the headteachers we interviewed were able to repeat the government's egalitarian claims for the National Curriculum policy, they were not able to provide evidence that their schools' new status had given or would give rise to significant curriculum reform, other than to draw attention to the fact that they now had more computers on site or new buildings to implement existing programmes of study. On the contrary, in the course of our visits to their schools, we were often struck by their reinvigorated traditionalism, and not just of the eight grammars within which we interviewed, which one might expect, but of many of the comprehensives as well. As further reported in Chapter 6, several had strengthened their dress codes and reinforced school uniform codes; others were giving increased emphasis to customary standards of pupil behaviour, including ways of approaching and addressing teachers; while at least one had banned the use of 'biros' in favour of fountain pens.

Summary and conclusion

The opting-out process is often initiated by headteachers anxious about the long-term security of their institutions, rather than by groups of parents or governors which have an increased sense of their own empowerment as 'consumers' of education. As a result, the GM schools policy in practice is sometimes more of a headteachers', than a parents' or governors', charter. Certainly, there are few signs that it increases either group's democratic control of schools. Indeed, once parents have taken part in the ballot, and approval for GM status is forthcoming, their involvement in their children's schools frequently exhibits no remarkable difference of emphasis from what they were used to previously. On the contrary, in some cases, headteachers of GM schools find they are able to exercise greater executive control without an equivalent increase in their sense of liability to either parents or governors. To that extent, the GM schools policy is capable of consolidating rather than undermining a specific 'producer' self-interest, although one that helps, rather than hinders, the implementation of the government's education reforms. The policy's heavy stress on the merits of *self*-governance encourages the headteachers of opted-out schools to celebrate a form of educational individualism. In practice, however, GM heads have limited room for manoeuvre because their activities are severely constrained by the central state, a chief concern of which is to affirm their role as key actors in the process of restructuring educational provision.

Financial advantage, rather than specifically educational considerations, weighs most heavily in headteachers' judgements of the merits of GM status. Headteachers, however, are sometimes unable to conceptualize more than a crude cause-and-effect relationship between extra funding, the quality of pupil learning and the raising of educational standards. Indeed, at the point of implementation, the GM schools policy confirms, rather than challenges, the assumption that extra resources are a necessary condition for school improvement, but in a way that articulates with traditional conceptions of schooling which mimic the government's implicit view of what counts as a 'good' education. How far and in what ways this mimicry is appreciated by parents and pupils that use GM schools is one of the issues discussed in the next chapter.

Chapter 5
Parents, Pupils and Grant-maintained Schools

Diversity, choice and parental participation

As we stressed in both the Introduction and Chapter 1, the GM schools policy is central to the government's strategy to extend parental choice. Although only one of several initiatives directed at this objective, opting out is regarded by its advocates as 'the "Jewel in the Crown" of parental power' (MacGregor, 1990). Moreover, despite shifts in the policy's objectives and changes to its administrative detail, the importance of GM status as a means of enhancing parental choice through restructuring and diversifying education provision has always been to the fore. To that extent, Patten's prediction in the 1992 Education White Paper that, 'by the next century, we will have achieved a system characterised not by uniformity but by choice, underpinned by the spread of grant-maintained schools', ought therefore to be seen as no more than a statement of what has been central to government thinking about education for some time.

The government envisages that the policy of 'freeing' schools from the constraints of LEA control will help them to become better managed and more responsive to the needs of parents who 'will enjoy enhanced influence over their conduct' (Rumbold, 1989). In addition, it is argued that opting out will foster healthy competition between all schools, including those in the private sector. It is claimed that such competition will lead to a general improvement in educational 'standards' and break down the barrier between public and private provision. GM schools, in other words, will become a 'half-way house' between state and independent schools, ending the existing unfairness of a system in which 'only the wealthy have choice' (Tebbit, 1987).

Critics, on the other hand, have suggested that the GM schools policy will lead to a two-tier system of education. For instance, Hilary Armstrong, a former Labour opposition spokesperson for education, has said that opting out 'celebrates and encourages divisions'. Others hostile to the policy have gone further arguing that it will lead to the reintroduction of selective schooling. Far from enhancing diversity and choice, opting out, they claim, will promote a new hierarchy of schools and limit opportunity.

Although it is too early to assess accurately the full impact of opting out, it is possible to explore whether the early experience of GM schools offers any indications that they are fulfilling the promises of their advocates or realizing the worst fears of their critics. Accordingly, this chapter examines the extent to which opting out diversifies school provision, expands parental choice and provides a new educational experience.

Research methods and data set

In addressing these issues we draw on data obtained from a set of interviews with pupils and parents that use eight opted-out secondary schools which, taken together, reflect the diversity of the GM sector as a whole. For comparative purposes, these data are complemented by information derived from a further set of interviews with parents and pupils using neighbouring LEA and independent schools in two selected areas (see Table 5.1 for details).

The pupil interviews were all conducted on school premises. At each school we sought to interview 40 pupils who were randomly selected from Years 7, 8 and 9. As well as asking pupils about their aspirations and family background, we enquired about their choice of school. In the GM schools, we were interested to know whether pupils had noticed any changes since the school opted out. It was on the basis of pupils' responses that we were able to identify two areas as examples of 'micro' education markets (Ball, 1992b). These markets are more fully discussed in the next chapter.

Table 5.1 *Number and type of pupil and parents interviewed*

	Schools	Pupils	Households	Parents
GM	8	264	106	129
LEA	4	124	56	65
Independent	2	72	20	22
Total	14	460	182	216

We then interviewed about one half of the pupils' parents in their homes. As well as gathering background information on their occupation, education and domestic arrangements, we asked them about the choice of secondary school for their child. With parents using a GM school we were concerned to find out either the extent to which the school's new status had been a factor in their choice, or whether opting out had increased their participation in the running of the school.

It is always difficult to ascertain the representativeness of a research sample. As both sets of interviews required parental permission and accessibility, the samples are to some extent opportunistic and thus likely to suffer from distortion. Certainly, our sample of parents contains a disproportionate number of middle-class households. Despite this limitation, the breadth and depth of the data as a whole enables us to begin to document parents' and pupils' experiences of opting out.

In the analysis which follows, we will employ Bowe, Ball and Gewirtz (1992) distinction between parents (and pupils) as 'choosers' and parents (and pupils) as 'users'. Although such categories are not mutually exclusive, they highlight the important difference between selecting a school, on the one hand, and the subsequent experience of that school, on the other.

GM schools: parents and pupils as 'choosers'

Supporters of opting out frequently argue that its 'success' can be measured through the national patterns of uptake (see Chapter 2) and the popularity of individual GM schools. Figures released by the Grant Maintained Schools Centre (GMSC) seem to confirm this 'success'. In

1991 it reported that 88 per cent of GM schools had boosted their rolls since opting out, with an average increase of 5.3 per cent (GMSC, 1991). This trend appears to have continued. At the end of the Summer Term 1992, the GMSC (1992a) claimed that 6 per cent of GM schools were full, with an average increase over the previous two years of 4.0 per cent. While we would not wish to argue that individual schools are not 'popular', our research does not indicate that they are 'successful' in terms of diversifying provision and extending parental choice.

To begin with, the designation 'grant-maintained' appears, as yet, to be of little consequence for parents and pupils choosing a secondary school. Of those parents who had selected a school after it had opted out (51/129), only eight felt that its new status had any bearing on their choice. Even here, the significance of 'opting out' was not usually perceived in terms of providing a 'new' choice, but of holding on to an 'old' one. As one parent put it: 'It was not important as such; what was important was that the school would be kept open'.

In Chapter 2 we argued that the opting out process is often initiated in reaction to, and with the aim of thwarting, an LEA reorganization plan entailing either closure or change of character. For such schools, opting out guarantees, at least in the short term, a secure future. Indeed, this increased security must be one factor behind the improved rolls mentioned earlier. On several occasions, parents drew our attention to their reluctance to select a school with an uncertain future. Pupils, too, noticed how numbers had increased once a 'threatened' school opted out. For example:

> Before, less people were coming here in case it closed. Now they know it isn't.... People aren't looking at us ... [and thinking] we're going to shut down.

To the extent that recruitment to a school is often adversely affected by plans to redesignate or close it, the security that GM status brings may well then reassure prospective parents.

Some parents, however, did refer to aspects of GM status beyond increased security as being relevant to their choice. One parent, for instance, felt that its novelty was important: 'It was a plus. Because it was new, they would be hot on the school'. Another said that that it must indicate a forward-looking approach: 'It shows a go ahead attitude, although I don't know a lot about it'. But for those few parents who saw the school's new status as a positive factor, there were as many who claimed to have selected a GM school *despite* it having opted out. These parents were either apprehensive about the ability of the school to 'go it alone', or worried about its possible isolation from other schools. As one mother remembered:

> My husband didn't want him [her son] to go – not because it's GM, but because of the LEA's attitude, like not playing football with the other schools would affect the kids.

Either way, the reasons why most parents choose GM schools seem little different from those which underlie the choice of any school. In fact, our research indicates that school selection tends to be grounded not on official designation, but on unofficial reputation gleaned from informal accounts. This holds true for all categories of school in which we interviewed, despite the higher public profile of many of the GM schools. Parents and pupils frequently construct a school's reputation through a combination of critical 'impressions' and anecdotal 'evidence'. The appearance and behaviour of pupils outside the school, for instance, is seen to be indicative of the qualities inside. Reference is typically made to the 'neatness' or 'scruffiness' of the uniform, to whether pupils could be seen swearing or smoking in the street, as well as more generalized aspects of their demeanour; for example: 'My father was a bus-driver and he always noted how good and well behaved the pupils were'. Anecdotal evidence usually comprises either accounts of individual successes (for instance: 'Our next-door neighbours' daughter went there and she did very well'), or 'revealing' incidents (eg, 'A friend who lives nearby got his nose broken there'). As discussed below, these informal accounts are often provided by close family and friends, but they also travel along quite circuitous routes. The following responses are typical, and come from GM, LEA and independent school respondents:

> My mum's bank manager told my dad that it is a very good school (GM pupil).
> Mum's friend used to be a dinner lady here (GM pupil).
> My parents knew about it from some people who lived down the road (LEA pupil).
> My brother was going to the school and he met our milkman who said his son was there and was really enjoying it ... (Independent pupil).

> When we were buying a house, everyone said 'Go to Queen Mary's' ... even the removal men said it was a good school (Independent pupil).

While most GM parents, like their LEA counterparts, went to open evenings and/or days and studied school prospectuses, one-quarter felt that it was the informal accounts which were the most useful in helping them to reach a decision. Furthermore, nearly 70 per cent of parents felt that the 'official' image presented by the school simply endorsed what they already knew through the local 'grapevine'.

The importance of family and friends as a key factor influencing the choice of a secondary school was a noticeable feature of *all* the maintained schools we researched. Specifically, 60 per cent of pupils report that the attendance of family members or friends played a central part in helping them to make up their mind about selecting a GM school, a similar proportion to that obtained from our interviews with pupils at LEA schools. Parent's responses endorse this. After the child's wishes, other parents and relatives were the most frequently mentioned influence.

Given that the GM schools in our sample had been operating under their new status for only a few terms, most of these informal accounts must stem from *pre*-GM status. Accordingly, the local confidence expressed through the popularity of a GM school appears to be founded less on the school's new status, but rather more on the preservation and continuity of its recent past.

The extent to which such popularity has been strengthened through opting out can be assessed through comparing 'first choice' incidence. Critics of the way in which LEAs 'override' parental preferences often argue that the removal of these 'restrictive' practices will enable more parents to realize a place at the school they would like. While other policies such as open enrolment and LMS also aim to 'empower' parents in this way, advocates of the GM schools policy anticipate that opted-out schools will particularly contribute to this process and be increasingly popular with parents who will 'queue up to get their children into each and every one of them' (MacGregor, 1990).

But do GM schools in fact contribute to a greater degree of 'first choice' realization? In other words, are GM schools the preferred option for those that use them more frequently than LEA schools? And if they are, can such a difference be explained in terms of opting out?

Ninety per cent of *all* the parents we spoke to claim that they were successful in terms of obtaining a place at the school of their first choice. There are, however, notable variations within the sample. All of the parents using independent schools say they achieved a place at the school of their choice, as did 93 per cent of GM parents. This was the case for only 79 per cent of LEA parents. Thus, over one-fifth of the parents we interviewed would have initially preferred their child to be at a different school.

Such figures might indicate that GM schools are seen as more desirable than LEA schools. Such a conclusion is hard to sustain, however. For a start, there are marked variations within each sector. While the *average* 'first choice' incidence is higher in the GM sector, individual LEA schools score *both* higher and lower. Second, even where 'first choice' incidence is higher in a school that has opted out, such popularity is not clearly connected with GM status. Comparison of 'first choice' incidence before and after opting out reveals a drop in frequency across *both* state sectors (Table 5.2). Ninety-five per cent of parents who selected a GM school prior to incorporation claim it was their 'first choice', compared to 92 per cent subsequently. While this is a less marked drop than reported by parents using LEA schools (88 per cent to 75 per cent), there is little indication of any change in the relative positions of schools in terms of perceived desirability. Indeed, the frequency with which first choices are attained by our sample as a whole declined from 93 per cent to 87 per cent since our research schools opted out. Although we would not wish to suggest that this reduction can be explained in terms of GM status, these figures do make it difficult to uphold the claim that opting out is leading to a greater realization of choice for parents.

In any event, the concept of 'choice' only has meaning if parents think there are feasible alternatives. When asked if they felt that they

Table 5.2 *First choice realization across sectors*

	Pre-GM (N = 75)	Post-GM (N = 107)
GM	95%	92%
LEA	88%	75%
Independent	100%	100%

did have a choice, 66 per cent of parents responded positively. It is important to note, however, that one-third felt that they did not have any choice. As with first choice incidence, most of those claiming not to have any choice are parents using local authority schools. Thus, while only 26 per cent of GM parents felt they had 'no choice', this was the case for 39 per cent of LEA parents. Again, though, it would not be reasonable to explain such a difference in terms of a school's opting out, inasmuch as for both the sample as a whole, and within particular sectors, there is little change in the perceived availability of 'choice' since GM status.

GM schools: parents and pupils as 'users'

While our research provides little indication that opting out has had any significant impact on expanding parental choice, it could still be argued that GM schools offer parents and pupils enhanced opportunities to influence the future of their schools over time, and thus to create choices not previously available. This is a particularly important argument which is sometimes used to combat the criticism that geographical constraints and the friction of distance inevitably impede and undermine parental choice. Choice, in this sense, is not conceived as operating between pre-existing alternatives, but rather in terms of the 'consumers' being able to effect longitudinal change within a single institution. As Baker (1988) once argued: 'We are offering choice in public service. We are offering choice to parents and governors who wish to exercise it to run their own schools'. It is in the light of this claim that we now want to examine whether GM schools are seen by their 'clients' to offer a different educational experience and greater participation.

There is certainly little doubt that the parents and pupils who took part in our research speak favourably of their GM experience. Eighty-three per cent of the parents we interviewed say they are 'very satisfied' with the educational provision for their children. Correspondingly, nearly all the GM pupils we spoke to consider that their school is the 'best' in the area; but then, so do their LEA and independent counterparts. Indeed, it was a feature of *all* the schools we visited that both pupils and parents feel warmly about the schools they or their children attend. Furthermore, comparisons of levels of expressed satisfaction before and after opting out reveal little change. Thus, however strongly parents support a school in its attempt to 'go it alone', opting out has not significantly transformed their experience of schooling. We certainly found no evidence to suggest that they feel themselves to have been 'liberated' from a situation in which 'their children [were] imprisoned in schools, in some cases in systems, ... totally repugnant to them' (Cormack, 1988).

Just as there is little difference between expressed satisfaction in a school, either since it opted out or between different kinds of school, neither is there any evidence to indicate that GM parents experience greater participation in the running of their school. Although 16 of the 55 parents we spoke to who had used the school prior to its opting out said that they now felt they had a greater sense of ownership, overall reported levels of parental involvement vary little with school type. In fact, more parents from LEA schools (54 per cent) claim to be involved with their children's schools than those using GM schools (44 per cent). Neither are there any significant changes in the reported level of involvement after a school has achieved GM status. In other words, there seems to be no relationship between the official status of a school and the degree of parental involvement.

Degrees of parental participation can also be explored through the extent to which parents are familiar with school governors. In other words, are parents using GM schools more likely to know any of members of the governing body since it opted out? Again, GM status does not seem to have wrought any expansion of familiarity. While 44 per cent of parents with pre-GM entrants claim they know at least one of the governor's names, only 26 per cent of post-GM parents did. The greater proportion of pre-GM familiarity might be explained in terms of the high profile of governors in the opt-out ballot. However, the overall level of awareness (35 per cent) is actually lower than that of their LEA counterparts, where 41 per cent of parents claim they are familiar with at least one governor, either in person or by name.

Similarly, pupil accounts do not reveal any significant alteration in their experience of schooling. Those differences that are evident are largely concerned with changes in 'resourcing' and 'rules'. In all of the GM schools in our sample, pupils highlight recent improvements to the fabric of their school and the purchase of new equipment. In many of the schools, they also report a tightening up of uniform and greater enforcement of 'traditional' modes of pupil behaviour. Despite these observations, they give little indication that their school is different 'in kind', either from its previous status or other state-maintained schools. Their school was, and remains, 'just an ordinary school'.

For most pupils, then, GM status is not thought of as marking a transformation, or even a transition. Indeed, in many GM schools, a significant number of pupils are unaware of any change in status. True, the degree of 'awareness' varies from school to school. Even so, nearly one-quarter of all the GM pupils we interviewed had no knowledge of any change in the management or status of their school. When pupils stated that they were aware that their school had opted out, they were often unsure as to what this implied. Many felt that it now meant the school was completely independent: 'It pays its own bills. It has got nothing to do with the government'. For these pupils, the significance of opting out was usually perceived in terms of the increased resourcing, and paradoxically, the pressure of 'standing up for yourself' (eg: 'The government doesn't give us money for things. We've got to raise it by sponsored things'). There was certainly little indication that 'going GM' had wrought any fundamental changes in their experience of state education. More often as not, it was seen to be 'just a change of name'. Another pupil put the same point in this way: 'There's nothing special about being grant-maintained ... 'cos most of the kids and teachers are still here'.

Summary and conclusion

Early perceptions of the GM schools policy indicate that opting out has had little significant impact on the choices parents and pupils make about schools and their experience of state education. In one sense this is hardly surprising given the constraints under which GM schools operate. Although the policy enables schools to 'break free of the local authority', it is an exaggeration to claim that this means these schools have been given 'full control of their own destinies' (Conservative Party, 1992), and for two reasons in particular. First, GM schools are obliged to teach the National Curriculum alongside their LEA counterparts which means that they are unable to devise distinctive curricula which might prove more attractive to parents seeking something different. And while, as we mention in Chapter 1, GM schools are to be encouraged to develop 'specialized' curricula, and even select on aptitude and ability a minority of their pupils, there is no suggestion that they will be able to do so outside the prescribed framework of the National Curriculum.

Second, on incorporation, GM schools are obliged to preserve their 'character'. Indeed, this is a precondition of 'going GM'. True, schools that opt out may apply for a subsequent change of character, but such changes must be argued for and are subject to the Secretary of State's approval. In any event, if we can rely on the findings of a survey recently conducted by the GMSC (1992a), it seems that most GM schools do not want to change their character.

It is hard, therefore, to see how GM schools can be said to be widening the education market through offering a 'new' alternative. It is perhaps useful at this point to contrast opting out with another government strategy for diversifying educational provision, namely, the CTC initiative. If, as Edwards, Gewirtz and Whitty (1992) argue, City Technology Colleges are 'obliged to be different', GM schools, it appears, are obliged to be the same. And, although some would claim that protecting existing alternatives is an important dimension of promoting choice, it does not constitute an *expansion* of choice. Thus far, then, it is only possible to argue that GM status represents preservation rather than innovation.

In this chapter, we have looked at the impact of opting out on parental choice and educational experience in a very general way. The analysis has largely consisted of comparing responses across sectors, and within sectors, between pre-GM and post-GM entrants. Although such an analysis is useful for looking at wider patterns, it glosses over differences between schools, and ignores the situationally specific way in which choices are made. In the next chapter, therefore, rather than look at the significance of GM schools across localities, we focus on two areas as examples of education markets.

Chapter 6
Opting Out and the Education Market

In the last chapter we compared the choices and perceptions of parents and pupils who use GM schools with those of their counterparts in LEA and independent schools. We argued that opting out has not yet become an important factor in choosing a school and that, on the whole, there seems to be little difference in the degree of parental involvement and nature of pupil experience in GM schools from that reported by those that use LEA schools. We also used cross-sector comparisons to show that opting out does not seem to have expanded parental choice.

While comparisons between sectors are important, they reveal little about the specific localities in which parents make choices. In this chapter, therefore, we focus on the impact of opting out in two areas which constitute 'education micro-markets'. By an 'education micro-market', we mean (following Ball, 1992b) a locality within which there are groups of schools between which there is either possible or actual competition for pupil enrolments. In the case of our research, the groups of schools concerned were identified from the responses of pupils in GM schools. In each of the areas which, for the purpose of anonymity, we have renamed 'Wellchester' and 'Milltown', the principal 'contenders' where we conducted research comprise two LEA comprehensives and one independent school.

Wellchester and Milltown: two micro-markets

Wellchester City (population 87,000) and Milltown (38,000) are located in the South of England. Although their size makes them unrepresentative of both large urban areas and rural regions, the limited, but diverse, number of schools from which parents and pupils could choose make them useful examples of the ways in which GM status affects school choice.

Wellchester schools

Bellevue, the first school to opt out in Wellchester, was incorporated in the GM sector in the summer term of 1990. A grammar school until reorganization, it now operates as an 11 to 18 boys' comprehensive. The occupational profile of *Bellevue* parents (as reported by pupils) stretches across all social classes, although there is an over-representation of both service- and intermediate-class parents. Out of the six maintained schools considered by our sample of *Bellevue* students, two schools in particular were mentioned more often than others, namely, *Canford School*, an 11 to 18 boys' comprehensive, and *Trelawney School*, an 11 to 18 co-educational comprehensive. Although both of these schools were secondary moderns until the 1972 reorganization took place, they draw from different kinds of catchment areas and have pupils from contrasting social class backgrounds (as defined by the Hope-Goldthorpe classification (see Goldthorpe and Hope, 1974) and in the Appendix). *Canford* is located next to a large council estate, and the parental occupations reflect this inasmuch as most are archetypical working class. *Trelawney*, on the other hand, is situated in a more prosperous part of the city and attracts pupils almost exclusively from the service class. Wellchester also has a thriving independent sector. In fact, one quarter of the pupils we interviewed are aware that their parents had considered a private school as an alternative. Of the independent sector, *Queen Mary's*, an 11 to 18 ex-direct grant boys' school, was the most frequently mentioned. Although it participates in the Assisted Places Scheme, our sample of pupils (which includes some with assisted places) came mainly from service-class backgrounds. Not one pupil has parents with working-class occupations.

Milltown schools

Stoneford High and *Merrick* are the two GM schools in Milltown on which we focused our research; they were both incorporated at the start of the 1990 academic year. *Stoneford High* remains an 11 to 18 girls' grammar school and *Merrick* is the neighbouring 11 to 18 boys' grammar. Although both retain selective admissions policies, despite successive reorganization attempts, the LEA had previously allocated children to the schools on the basis of proximity as well as test results. Since opting out, this has been abandoned. In both schools, our sample of pupils come disproportionately, although by no means exclusively, from service- and intermediate-class households. The two LEA schools which were mentioned most often by our GM pupil respondents are *Arneside*, an 11 to 18 co-educational comprehensive, and *Midlane*. Until 1990, *Midlane* was designated a 'secondary modern' school. Since then it has become 'comprehensive', though it has lost its sixth form provision. The legacy of its recent status, and the working-class neighbourhood in which it is located, is reflected in the low number of service-class parents which use it, particularly those of a higher professional grade. Most of the parents of our pupil sample have occupations within the intermediate- and working-class categories. The independent sector serving Milltown comprises only one school, *Woodcote*, a co-educational school with both day and boarding provision. Like *Queen Mary's* in Wellchester, *Woodcote* offers assisted places. Similarly, though, our sample was almost exclusively drawn from the service class.

In the following section, we explore the extent to which the patterns of choice we looked at in the last chapter are reflected in Milltown and Wellchester. We then assess whether opting out has impacted on the class compositions of schools in these localities and consider the future directions along which the reputations of schools are being constructed.

First-choice realization

In the last chapter we saw how there was a drop in the number of parents achieving a place at the school of their choice and that this was highest for those parents using LEA schools. This pattern is repeated in

Table 6.1 *First-choice realization in Wellchester state schools*

	Pre-GM (N = 13)	Post-GM (N = 27)
Bellevue (GM)	100%	90%
Trelawney (LEA)	100%	100%
Canford (LEA)	100%	71%

Milltown and Wellchester, although there are marked variations both between the two areas and between individual schools.

Among our Wellchester parents, there was a slight decrease in the achievement of first-choice school, from 100 per cent to 93 per cent. However, this decrease is not uniformly spread, nor does it simply reflect sector differences (Table 6.1).

Trelawney has remained a 'first-choice' school for all the parents with whom we spoke. While *Canford* might appear to have declined in 'desirability', the actual numbers of parents involved are few. It is also worth noting the directions of 'first-choice' for 'disappointed' parents. In every case, *Trelawney* was mentioned as the preferred school, rather than *Bellevue*.

In Milltown, there is a different pattern. Again, the number of parents reporting success in gaining a place at the school of their choice declined from 91 per cent to 78 per cent, but with more marked contrasts (Table 6.2).

In Milltown, the GM schools clearly have not seen the same drop in first-choice admissions as the LEA schools. However, the relative positions of the schools remain unchanged since *Merrick* and *Stoneford* opted out. *Midlane*, for instance, which to some extent was always a

Table 6.2 *First-choice realization in Milltown state schools*

	Pre-GM (N = 32)	Post-GM (N = 34)
Stoneford High (GM)	100%	100%
Merrick (GM)	90%	100%
Arneside (LEA)	100%	85%
Midlane (LEA)	67%	40%

'second choice', still remains so, despite its formal redesignation from 'secondary modern' to 'comprehensive'. What does appear to have been affected is the degree of differentiation, which has increased quite substantially. Given that both *Stoneford High* and *Merrick* are grammar schools which have strengthened their admissions procedures since opting out, it is more likely that the drop in the number of parents gaining their first-choice school stems not from GM status, but from the articulation of opting out in these cases with selective schooling. Nevertheless, not all the 'disappointed' parents preferred the GM schools to others. While nearly two-thirds of them would have initially liked their children to go to the grammar schools, over one-third originally chose another LEA school. *Arneside* was named as the first-choice school by *Midlane* parents almost as frequently as *Stoneford High* or *Merrick*. Either way, the most that one can say from such figures is that GM status has consolidated existing patterns of first-choice preference, rather than altered the relative positions either between or within sectors.

Perceptions of choice

Parental perceptions of the degree of choice have also been affected at Milltown. There is a marginal increase in the proportions of parents using the selective GM schools who claim they have a choice of school. Indeed, it is the *Merrick* and *Stoneford High* parents who, out of all the state schools we visited, are the most likely to say they have 'choice'. There is, however, a corresponding decrease in the range of choices which the LEA parents perceive as available.

Parents using *Midlane* and *Arneside* are more likely to say they have 'no choice', both before, but particularly after, the two schools opted out. Parents who claim they have no choice mention two main impediments. Some report that the 11+ equivalent has deprived their child of entry to the school they want. Others feel that the mere existence of such testing denies them any choice. As one *Arneside* parent put it: 'I don't have a choice because I choose to send my children to a comprehensive. And because there's a grammar school next door, *Arneside* can't be comprehensive'. Again, however, it appears to be the connection between GM and selective status that is the most significant variable.

That GM status, by itself, does not alter perceptions of available choice is evident from our study of Wellchester where there is little change in the number of parents claiming to have 'choice' either before, or after, *Bellevue* opted out.

State and private schooling

There is no indication from either Milltown or Wellchester that GM schools have been able to blur the boundary between state and private schooling. Although parents using the GM sector are likely to have considered independent alternatives more frequently than their LEA counterparts (36 per cent as opposed to 16 per cent), such a pattern is more likely to be explained by the conjuncture of GM and selective status rather than by GM status itself. In any event, there is no change in the proportion of parents looking to the independent sector before and after opting out.

School choice and social class

Critics of the GM schools policy often argue that it is not just the question of 'choice' that is at stake, but the way in which choice is socially distributed. They claim that, while there may be enhanced opportunities for some, they will be diminished for others. The chair of the Association of Metropolitan Authorities, for example, predicted that opting out will lead to 'a grab by middle class parents of their share of education at the expense of working class parents' (Fletcher, 1988). Walford and Miller (1991) also consider that increasing differences between schools will contribute, not to diversity, but to hierarchy, 'with the private sector at the head, the CTCs and GM schools next, and the various locally managed LEA schools following' (p 165). It is also feared that this ranking will reflect and reinforce existing patterns of socio-economic stratification (Edwards and Whitty, 1992).

To what extent are such processes at work in our two 'micro-markets'? We explore this question from three directions: incidence of first choice realization, perceptions of choice, and changes in the social class compositions of the schools.

In neither Wellchester nor Milltown is it possible to argue that there is a clear class dimension to the frequency with which parents are able to secure a place at the school of their choice. In both areas, households where the father is not in paid employment are the least likely to have gained access to a preferred school, whether GM or LEA. While households where either a father or mother has a service-class occupation are the most likely to be successful in this direction, fewer intermediate-class parents realize their 'first-choice' school than working-class parents. Accordingly, while we acknowledge that the distortion and size of our sample makes it impossible to draw any firm conclusions, we have no evidence to indicate that opting out effects any discernable shift in the relationship between first-choice realization and socio-economic status.

On the other hand, there do seem to be differences in the way in which 'choice' is experienced by households from different social-class backgrounds. Thus, while parents with service-class occupations are as likely to say they have 'no choice' as working-class parents, the professional parent who selects an independent school 15 miles away from home has a higher number of possible options than the working-class parent who must rely on state-maintained provision within close proximity and whose child is unable to gain access to the school they prefer. It appears that as the number of available alternatives is enhanced through higher socio-economic status, so their acceptability decreases. As discussed earlier, GM status, by itself, does not increase the 'acceptability' of state education for those using the private sector. Equally, neither does it expand the perceived range of choices available to those dependent on state provision.

Comparison of the occupations of parents reveals that there are differences in the social-class composition of schools. In both 'micro-market' areas, the two schools with the lowest first-choice incidence, *Canford* and *Midlane*, are also those located in working-class areas and used predominantly by parents with working-class occupations. The occupational profile of parents using the GM schools, that is, *Bellevue*, *Stoneford High* and *Merrick*, have a higher representation of professional and intermediate classes. However, this should not lead one to conclude that in our two 'micro-markets' GM schools are the dominant type of school for middle-class parents. Both *Trelawney* and *Arneside*, the two 'popular' LEA schools in our market areas, attract parents whose socio-economic status is as high, if not higher, than the neighbouring GM school.

With the exception of the independent schools, whose parents (particularly fathers) are drawn predominantly from the professional class, there appears to be no inevitable correlation between the status of the school, whether LEA, GM, comprehensive or selective, and its social-class composition. Nor are there any statistically significant shifts in social-class composition since opting out. Thus, the sample of parents whose children attend *Merrick*, the boys' GM grammar school, shows a decrease in professional households since opting out, despite the strengthening of selection procedures. At *Bellevue*, on the other hand, there is a slight increase in their representation.

In summary, while acknowledging both the weaknesses of our own sample and the limitations of using occupational categories as an indicator of social class, particularly for women, comparison of parents' occupations (both mothers' and fathers') reveals that there has been little alteration in social composition either between types of school or between individual schools. Although there are marked variations between schools, these do not reflect sector differences, independent parents excepted. In both Wellchester and Milltown, the neighbouring LEA schools seem to have social-class compositions both higher and lower than the GM school. Nor do we have any indication of a change in the occupational location of parents using GM schools since they opted out.

GM status and reputation management

The degree to which schools are able to move 'upmarket' is likely to depend on the extent to which they can reformulate their unofficial reputations. For, as we argued in the last chapter, official accounts and designations of schools are less important than informal perceptions.

There seems little doubt that state schools are now more conscious that the management of their reputation is a central aspect of attracting parents. All schools are concerned to 'market' themselves through the presentation of glossy prospectuses and open days/evenings. There also appears to be a renewed emphasis on school uniform as an outward sign of discipline. Pupils in nearly all the state-maintained schools that we visited commented on recent changes in the reinforcement of school rules and efforts to improve the appearance and fabric of buildings. This was particularly marked, however, in those schools which had opted out. In every one of the GM schools within which we did research, pupils made unprompted comments on improvements in decorative order and resourcing since opting out. At *Bellevue*, for instance, pupils noticed new science and sports equipment, new computers, new carpets, new lighting and general decorative improvements to both buildings and grounds. All this was evidence, as one pupil put it, of 'lots more money'. Girls at *Stoneford High* made similar comments, referring to 'lots of decorating' and 'more money for facilities, new books and more PE equipment', as well as new buildings, such as a resource centre. *Merrick* had undergone similar refurbishment. Boys there mentioned new technology and science block, additional equipment and general redecoration.

Although, as we stressed in the last chapter, official school presentations usually confirm, rather than alter, parents' perceptions of the desirability of a school, the importance of impressions gained on initial visits is still significant. The number of computers, in particular, which all of the GM schools have substantially increased, is frequently mentioned by parents, reflecting Ball, Gewirtz and Bowe's (1992) impression that 'these machines ... symbolize something important'. Improvements in resourcing and attention to decorative order are more than likely, then, to help foster positive impressions and augment school recruitment.

GM schools are also actively engaged in more subtle areas of 'reputation management'. Increasing emphasis, for example, is being placed on pupils' appearance and behaviour as indicators of good schooling. The headteacher of *Bellevue*, for instance, highlights the need to 'redefine' his school's image:

> I think it had become distinctly blurred at the edges. We've sharpened the whole thing up with the emphasis on our traditions and values; the good manners; children standing up when a visitor goes into the classroom; insistence on uniform being worn; insistence on good manners being shown not only in school but outside school as well; emphasis on high academic standards.

These changes, while mainly cosmetic in character, are often writ large in the perceptions and experiences of the pupils they affect. *Bellevue* pupils make frequent reference to the tightening up of old rules and the introduction of new ones. Mention was made, for instance, of the attention being paid to pupils leaving the top button of their shirt undone under their tie. Pupils also report that they are required to use 'Sir' or

'Miss' when talking to staff. As one pupil said: 'they've come all heavy on politeness'.

These experiences are also echoed in *Merrick* and *Stoneford High*, where, for example, pupils feel that since the school opted out, their appearance has come under increasing scrutiny. The following is a typical comment: 'Recently they've clamped down on uniform, like no black socks or tights. It's grey everything'.

The greater degree to which these changes are manifest since a school opted out may reflect the extent to which GM status, and the greater independence and better funding which it brings, enables schools to highlight their 'otherness' from neighbouring LEA schools. The next section draws on pupil perceptions of 'opting out' to examine whether this sense of 'otherness' is beginning to filter through into the local grapevine.

Pupil perceptions of opting out

There is evidence to suggest that the kind of superficial differences mentioned above are being transformed into more significant differences both for those who use GM schools and for their LEA counterparts. Although on the 'inside' of a GM school, the content of its curriculum and the composition of its pupils remain unchanged, its 'outside' relations are altered, a process which is likely to be exacerbated where opting out brings isolation from neighbouring LEA schools. At *Bellevue*, in particular, pupils indicate an awareness of becoming 'different' from other state schools:

> It does make it seem different, I don't know how, but when people speak about it, it just makes you feel different though it hasn't really changed.
> In conversation with people you feel really proud of the 'GM' title. As a pupil, though, I think nothing is really different.
> In relation to other schools, it probably does make a difference, but inside, not much.

The sense of 'difference' is also apparent in the responses of pupils who attend neighbouring LEA schools. Most of these pupils are unaware of their neighbour's new status, and therefore unable to define what 'GM' means. On the other hand, for those who were able to respond, GM status is clearly connected with being 'different' from 'ordinary' schools. In Wellchester, for instance, there is an evident association between 'opting out' and 'going private'. These varied comments from *Canford* pupils clearly indicate that *Bellevue* is no longer 'one of ours':

> They're out of it – like if they want to buy something they have to use their own money instead of the council's.
> Some schools the council pays for, but they (GM schools) have to raise money for the things they want.
> They pay their own way. They don't get any funding from the government.
> It's when they don't want to be run by the government and have things like the National Curriculum.

The dimensions along which the differences between GM and 'ordinary' schools are constructed often magnify the particular properties of the nearby GM school. In Milltown, for instance, GM status is seen to be commensurate with single-sex, selective schooling, as well as private education. In this connection, *Arneside* and *Midlane* pupils made the following comments about GM status:

> Grant-maintained means a school is single sex, not mixed.
> Grant-maintained means you've got to be brainy to go there.
> It's something to do with opting out of the National Curriculum.
> You have to pay money to go there.
> It's when a school goes private.

For these pupils, the designation 'GM' clearly denotes something other than 'ordinary' state education. As one respondent from *Arneside* put it: 'Grant-maintained means they don't do the things everybody else does'.

Interestingly, although pupils at independent schools are similarly confused over the precise characteristics of GM status, they are in no doubt that, whatever else it stands for, it does not denote 'private'. *Queen Mary's* and *Woodcote* pupils, for instance, claim that opting out means:

> It doesn't get any money from the government. But it's not a private school.
> The government keeps it going.

It's a state school, but they've opted out of the government system. It's opted out of the government and it's trying to cope on its own. But it stays a state school.

They don't want to do the National Curriculum and are paid for by the state.

Unlike their LEA counterparts, pupils at independent schools, like their parents, perceive GM schools as being firmly located within the state sector. Accordingly, taken together, both sets of interpretations suggest that opting out has some way to go before it can lay claim to have effected a blurring of the perceived boundary that distinguishes state from private schooling.

Summary

What, then, do the experiences of pupils and parents in Milltown and Wellchester reveal about GM schools in the marketplace and the possible consequences of opting out on secondary provision?

So far there is not much to indicate that GM status, by itself, is having any significant impact on patterns of school choice in either locality. Certainly, it marks neither a widening of choice, nor a highly desired alternative. There is evidence, however, that the conjuncture of GM status and selective schooling alters the ability of parents to obtain a place at the school of their choice. The experience of parents and pupils in Milltown indicates that, with the exception of those both willing and able to secure a grammar school place, GM status frustrates, rather than furthers, the realization of choice.

Such effects, however, are fairly localized. There are no grounds to suggest that the GM schools policy is leading to the widespread return of a selective system of secondary education. As discussed in Chapter 2, the high proportion of grammar schools within the GM sector is likely to diminish as both the number of schools opting out increases and the available pool of selective schools becomes incorporated. On the other hand, it is possible that GM schools, both through their more vigorous reputation management, and the renewed emphasis on 'traditional' values, may be able to foster an image of themselves as the hallmark of 'quality' state schooling. Despite the wide diversity of GM secondary schools, it seems feasible that the high proportion of selective and ex-grammar schools within the GM sector will help to foster a corporate identity which, by association, will augment the reputations of what might otherwise be considered 'ordinary' schools (compare, for instance, Edwards, Fitz and Whitty, 1989 on the impact of the Assisted Places Scheme on 'minor' independent schools). These associations are likely to be strengthened by the frequency with which 'grant-maintained' status is confused in ordinary parlance with 'direct-grant' schooling.

Such impressions are likely to be further endorsed through formal sector comparisons. In his 1991 Annual Report, the former Senior Chief Inspector of Schools, for instance, stated that standards in GM schools are 'rather higher than in the maintained sector as a whole' (DES, 1992). Such deceptive comparisons are also likely to be increasingly put forward on the basis of unqualified analysis of published examination results. Already, for example, the GM Schools Centre (1992a) claims that 60 per cent of opted-out schools achieve above the national average scores for GCSE grades.

Even if GM schools do become perceived as 'beacons' of excellence, it is unclear what implications opting out will have on educational provision and the distribution of educational opportunities. Our evidence does not suggest that GM schools are likely to become the prevalent form of provision for middle-class parents. In both our 'micro-markets', for instance, the GM emphasis on traditional imagery as the epitome of 'good' schooling is not universally sought after. Indeed, *Trelawney* and *Arneside* market themselves along 'progressive' lines and appear to retain higher than average proportions of pupils from service- and intermediate-class households. It would seem, therefore, that, in some cases, certain sections of the middle class retain an allegiance to particular forms and orientations of LEA-maintained comprehensive education.

Such qualifications should not be interpreted to suggest that GM schools will contribute to a diversity based on parity of esteem. Rather, they illustrate that patterns of choice are complex and situationally specific. While our data do not indicate that the worst fears of the GM schools policy's critics are being realized, neither do they suggest that their concerns should be disregarded. Certainly, there is evidence that opting out preserves and pronounces existing differences between schools. Although the implications of a consolidation of differences are not easy to predict, the accounts of parents and pupils in Wellchester and Milltown make it hard to sustain the claim made by the policy's advocates that GM schools will expand parental choice and offer a new experience of state education.

Chapter 7
The Policy's Long-term Implications

Introduction

The 1992 Education White Paper, *Choice and Diversity: A New Framework for Schools* (DfE, 1992a), makes clear the government's intention to augment the GM schools policy, and thus enhance a process which, it claims, is 'transforming the educational landscape of this country'. Commencing with the White Paper, this chapter critically examines the government's proposals to establish GM schools as 'the natural organizational model for schools provision'. In particular, it explores the larger significance of mass opting out in terms of its implications for the government of education and the future character of school services. The final part of the chapter reviews some issues that parents and governors need to take into account when considering GM status for their schools.

The 1992 Education White Paper

Although the White Paper was published in July 1992, many education commentators had anticipated most of its key features earlier that summer. Certainly, very little of what emerged came as a surprise. Writ large in the document is the government's determination to expand the number of GM schools as rapidly as possible.

The specific proposals contained in the White Paper include:

- the creation of a new statutory body, The Funding Agency for Schools (FAS), to be responsible, in all cases, for funding and auditing GM schools and, in others, where specific circumstances prevail, for providing, either alongside or independent of LEAs, sufficient school places for a particular area;
- measures to make the transition to GM status easier for schools;
- mechanisms to allow a school opting out simultaneously to apply for a change in size or character;
- coupling GM status with further steps to increase specialization and diversity in schools;
- procedures to facilitate the creation of new GM schools by voluntary agreement;
- providing the opportunity for small schools to opt out via 'cluster' arrangements.

These new initiatives are accompanied by a striking increase in the powers of the Education Secretary to regulate even more aspects of the school service. Correspondingly, local authorities will lose, incrementally, many of their statutory duties and functions as the FAS assumes its planning powers. It is these aspects of the White Paper to which many educationalists and others drew most critical attention when it was published. The Association of Metropolitan Authorities, for example, interpreted the White Paper as heralding 'massive centralization', while *The Times* saw its measures as leading to the 'nationalization of schools'. Taking a slightly different, but equally pessimistic, tack, the Labour Party accused the government of 'rigging the system' to encourage more schools to opt out. In similar vein, Eric Bolton, a former Chief Inspector of Schools, said that the White Paper's proposals would lead to popular opted-out schools choosing pupils rather than parents choosing schools. The GM Schools Centre, on the other hand, predictably welcomed the new funding agency which it believed would 'provide stability of funding whilst having a light touch'. Against the background of these competing claims made about the changes proposed in the White Paper, we want to examine them in more detail, beginning with the FAS.

The Funding Agency for Schools

The creation of a statutory body to oversee important aspects of the administration of opting out is the government's preferred means of resolving several issues which had arisen as the number of GM schools increased. It can also be interpreted as a way for ministers and officials to square a circle in relation to the continued preferential funding of GM schools while, concurrently, reducing the overall costs of the policy. As we noted in Chapter 1, the government is committed to extra funding for GM schools at levels which recognize their averred increased responsibilities – a coded way of saying they will continue to be better resourced than neighbouring LEA schools. At the same time, however, concern has been expressed about the size, likely administrative costs and capacity of a central bureaucracy to oversee effectively an expanded and expanding GM sector. The character and proposed functions of the FAS are devised to address these difficulties.

As it is represented in the White Paper, and subsequently confirmed in the 1993 Education Act, the FAS is a ministerially appointed body, comprising 10 to 15 members, which is delegated responsible for the funding and regulation of the GM sector. FAS members are 'drawn from various backgrounds to reflect a broad mix of education and other experience'. The Agency's budget and staffing are reviewed on an annual basis by the Secretary of State, who is also responsible for appointing its chief executive.

In the first instance, the FAS assumes responsibilities for paying grants to, and monitoring the financial expenditure of, GM schools, thus relieving the DfE of these tasks. Its functions expand as the number of GM schools increases, which means that its involvement in planning the supply of school places will be on an authority-by-authority basis. Indeed, its participation in planning and provision is only triggered at the point when 10 per cent of secondary or primary pupils in an LEA are enrolled in GM schools. This is the so-called 'entry point', at which moment the Agency begins to share with a local authority the duty to secure sufficient places for all pupils entitled to a full-time education. In this connection, it is worth recalling that in Chapter 2 we estimate that over 40 LEAs are presently in the process of losing up to 10 per cent of their secondary schools to the GM sector.

Once involved, the FAS assumes other very considerable powers. For example, it is able:

- to instigate the establishment of new schools;
- to propose or agree enlargement or change in character of existing GM schools;

- to share with LEAs responsibility for securing places for pupils with a statement of special educational needs.

The Agency is also expected to act in concert with LEAs to co-ordinate the orderly transfer of students from primary to secondary schools and to seek the rationalization of school places where these are in excess of pupil numbers. In relation to education planning, these shared arrangements continue up to the point where 75 per cent of secondary or primary pupils are being educated in opted-out schools.

At this so-called 'exit point', it is intended that LEAs should relinquish *all* planning functions to the Agency. Once this point is reached, local authorities, in effect, cease to have responsibility for the organization of education within their administrative boundaries, although they retain a number of statutory duties, including responsibility for the special educational needs of some children, providing welfare and psychological services for others and enforcing school attendance.

The FAS has responsibility not only for the administration of the GM sector, but for most matters relating to the planning and provision of school education, including all closures, amalgamations and redesignations. The White Paper, however, anticipates that some LEAs may wish to transfer their planning functions to the FAS before the 'exit point' is achieved. Accordingly, the 1993 Education Act provides the Education Secretary with the necessary powers to enable this to happen.

The duties assumed by the FAS clearly signal the incremental demise of LEAs in their current form. Under the 1944 Education Act, the LEA's basic duty is to secure the provision of efficient primary and secondary education in sufficient schools. The 1993 Education Act considerably modifies this requirement. It includes, for example, measures that repeal the statutory duty for local authorities to establish education committees. While there is no suggestion that the post of Chief Education Officer or Director of Education should be abolished under the Act, it may be unnecessary for local authorities to have committees of elected members specifically charged to oversee the education of children. The present form of public accountability which exists between schools and elected representatives, and which was established in 1944, is therefore likely to be brought to an end in many parts of the country within the next few years.

Critical commentary on the FAS has focused on two areas: its implications for education planning, and its likely role in reshaping the structures of the government of education. In the medium term, there is a concern that chaos and confusion may result from arrangements in which two public bodies – LEAs and the FAS – are vested with responsibilities for educational planning. As we report in Chapter 3, matching school places and pupil numbers is a complex and politically sensitive task, and never more so than when the fate of a school is involved. In this connection, all local officials will confirm that closing one or more schools always entails a long and expensive period of consultation. Not surprisingly, the same officials are doubtful that the new arrangements, involving as they do two bodies with divergent aims, will make this task any easier.

Even after the FAS assumes full responsibility for education planning, there remain at least two unresolved difficulties. The first concerns the quality and amount of resources the FAS will have at its disposal to make decisions about the kinds and distribution of schools which local communities require. As Maclure (1992) comments, such decisions have been customarily based on a variety of information, including demographic, infrastructural and employment data, as well as details about the performance and effectiveness of schools. Maclure and others are understandably anxious that, unlike existing LEAs, the FAS may not have the staff or expertise to collect, collate and analyse this sort of material in order to reach informed judgements in education planning.

The second major educational concern is the relationship between the FAS and local communities. Although it is anticipated that the work of the FAS will be undertaken by regional offices, these are likely to be few in number as compared with LEAs, and therefore somewhat remote from the schools and those parents directly affected by their planning decisions. Moreover, in the absence of a tier of elected local representatives, it is not clear to whom parents can turn if they are dissatisfied with the schooling arrangements made by the Agency, other than the local ombudsman (Bogdanov, 1992).

The composition of the FAS and its regional offices will be directly, and indirectly, determined by ministers. The composition of the FAS and its satellite offices may well, therefore, carry significant implications for the character of schooling fostered in the 1990s. Given that the FAS has no obligation to be accountable to, or to meet, or even ascertain, the declared needs of local communities, and given too the likely preferences and prejudices of its government-appointed members, it will be in a powerful position to promote the mix and variety of schools wanted by the Education Secretary. In effect, the FAS could function as a mechanism for the promotion of specialization in education and a return to academic selection; it may even play a key role in determining whether, and at what pace, religious bodies will receive support to establish their own schools. The FAS's lines of accountability, and its possible role in the restructuring of education, thus raise important constitutional issues which, in the rush to celebrate the supposed positive attributes of GM status for schools, tend to be either obscured or overlooked.

The establishment of the FAS will replace the oversight of education by locally elected representatives with ministerially appointed non-elected quangos. This alone represents an important shift of power and control away from the periphery to the centre. For while the FAS consolidates 'the constitutional principle of ministerial responsibility' (Bogdanov, 1992), it does so in such a way that enhances the power of ministers to drive forward their policy preferences through executive agencies, the membership of which is appointed by, and accountable to, central government.

Thus, although such bodies certainly facilitate the implementation of ministerial preferences, there remains the threat of administrative overload at the centre. As the appointed agencies emerge as executive arms of central power, then Whitehall is likely to be held directly responsible for deficiencies, however small, in education. In the long term, these arrangements may therefore be less efficient in handling local difficulties than the administration which preceded them. In general, then, the FAS can be interpreted as an initiative, to be seen alongside others of a similar kind promoted by the government, which will help to create a 'new magistracy'; that is to say, a new, non-elected élite that assumes increasing responsibility for local governance without being accountable to local populations (Stewart, 1992).

Funding the GM sector

We noted in Chapter 1 the growing dilemma facing the government in connection with the rising costs of opting out. Essentially, this dilemma centres on how to maintain the financial attractions associated with GM status in order to encourage more and more schools to opt out, while, at the same time, accommodating the Treasury's concern to control the overall cost of the policy. It is against this background that the White Paper promulgates measures intended to modify existing financial arrangements.

The most prominent initiative is the introduction of a Common Funding Formula (CFF) for GM schools to be introduced on a phased basis in authorities 'where there are sufficient primary or secondary schools to justify it'. The CFF is related to the government's Standing Spending Assessment (SSA). Based on pupil numbers and other social factors, the SSA represents the government's estimate of how much grant a particular LEA requires to run its school service. The SSA for an LEA will be split between its schools and those that have opted out of its control. The total of the CCF within an LEA will thus be a share of the authority's SSA.

By employing SSAs as the starting point in calculating the amount of grant to be made available to GM schools, the government is effectively reproducing the differences in resourcing that currently prevail between GM schools in different areas of the country (Travers, 1993). Certainly, it broadly preserves the relatively high central grants made to inner-city GM schools.

While the government's proposals for funding GM schools go some way towards achieving administrative simplicity, two concerns in particular have been expressed about them. On the one hand, they fail to register or reflect the fact that more than half of all the local authorities in England spend more than their proposed SSAs on education. In LEAs where this is the case, existing GM schools would, therefore, be subject to a substantial reduction in their funding. On the other hand, some GM schools within LEAs that underspend could benefit considerably to the extent that the application of the CCF will secure for them a fixed proportion of the original SSA.

Potentially more embarrassing for a government committed to encouraging schools to opt out is the confusion caused in relation to schools considering GM status. From details in the White Paper and subsequent press commentary, schools were unable to calculate what the financial benefits and disbenefits would be if they opted out. Because of these confusions, the DfE quickly drafted interim measures (DfE, 1992b, 1992c) which link levels of funding for 1993/4 to existing 1992/3 LEA budget decisions. While, therefore, both the GM schools presently operating and the schools wanting to opt out during this and next year can, on this basis, roughly calculate the sums of money to which they can look forward, some of the LEAs that will be affected are less than happy. They argue that, because schools which leave their control and become GM are given a budget based on their LMS formulae, the decision to link future funding with current budget decisions will have the effect of constraining their wish to delegate further sums of money to schools that do not want to opt out. As Rogers (1993) argues: 'Thus, ironically, the possibly over-zealous encouragement of one government policy (affecting ... only a small minority of schools) could lead to a marked inhibition of another (affecting all schools)'. Relatedly, there are fears that these interim proposals will result in some GM schools being allocated monies in lieu of services which in fact LEAs have scrapped and put into their main LMS budgets. In other words, GM schools could be paid twice for the same services – once in their LMS-based grant, and again in their additional funding (Pyke, 1993).

Even so, both the White Paper and the subsequent consultation documents indicate that the government is likely to reduce the amounts of some existing grants. In particular, the DfE has given a strong indication that transitional awards will be reduced substantially. In addition, it has issued advice about the kinds of initiatives it will be prepared to support through 'named project' capital grants which, in future, must relate to health and safety, major repairs or ones designed to meet changing educational needs.

Easing the transition to GM status

The White Paper also outlines a series of measures designed to remove particular barriers to further progress in the scale and pace of opting out. These include the abolition of the need for a second, 'resolution meeting' of governors, prior to proceeding to a ballot of parents. This proposal, the government believes, will have the effect of reducing avoidable delays. In addition, and to ease the burden on primary schools contemplating GM status, small schools will require only a relatively small number of people to form a governing body.

The White Paper also consolidates the government's criticism of the sort of tactics allegedly used by some LEAs to discourage schools from seeking GM status, which it has variously described as unfair, sometimes misleading, and occasionally intimidatory. The government wants to limit LEA campaign expenditure so that local authorities are able to issue no more than one leaflet to parents prior to a ballot on opting out. This has to be set alongside the government's increasing use of press releases to challenge the veracity of claims made by LEAs in opting-out campaigns and requests for the LEAs concerned to justify the positions they take (DfE, 1992d). The London Borough of Merton has recently been subject to this form of challenge. In other respects, however, it also indicates that the government is becoming increasingly frustrated that its message about the advantages of GM status is not getting across in ways which convince parents to pursue opting out.

One of the more important measures in the White Paper relates specifically to small rural primary schools. In the light of the special administrative difficulties they are likely to face as autonomous institutions, small schools are now able to opt out in 'clusters' and to be governed by a single body. For the purposes of the ballot, however, each school must conduct its own, and a majority of parents in favour of opting out is required in all the schools involved before the cluster can apply as a whole for GM status.

All these measures register the government's determination to create a GM sector embracing all or most state schools. Indeed, because the government believes that some governing bodies block discussion of opting out, all of them are now required to deliberate on the issue each year. Moreover, schools which choose to stay with their education authority must explain their decision in the governors' annual report to parents (Hymas, 1993). Even though the Education Secretary has drawn back from introducing compulsory ballots in all LEA schools, the prescriptive nature of these proposals undermines considerably the original enabling character of the GM schools policy.

Along with most of the other measures in the White Paper, they also, as we have stressed repeatedly, help to weaken further the present role of LEAs. Indeed, the 1993 Education Act puts into statutory form the government's intention to create an education system in which local authorities have only a minimal part to play. To that extent, it is necessary at this point in our analysis to qualify the more optimistic estimates of their future with which we concluded Chapter 3.

The White Paper and the future of LEAs

There is no doubt that LEAs, individually and collectively, have lost many duties, powers and functions as the result of legislation between 1987 and now. They include:

- the ability to settle by national collective bargaining the pay and other main conditions of employment of 400,000 teachers, most of whom are their employees;
- significant financial discretion as a consequence of the requirement that they must delegate to schools up to 85 per cent of their potential budgets;
- the power to regulate school admissions and plan school provision accordingly;
- the capacity to take the lead in the professional development of teachers following the requirement by the DfE that much of the specific grant for inservice training be devolved to schools.

The losses can also be calculated in strictly financial terms if one considers the £1 billion lost upon the transfer of the polytechnics out of local government and the literal decimation (£2 billion from £20 billion) of LEA expenditure consequent upon the government's decision to take mainstream further education out of local authority control.

The White Paper and the 1993 Education Act compound the problems facing LEAs. Beyond the statutory minimum of services they are obliged to go on providing (welfare and psychological services, boarding facilities where appropriate, and home-to-school transport), the government expects the rest, such as those affecting peripatetic music tuition, school libraries, leisure facilities, inspections and payroll, to be 'purchased' mostly from the private sector. LEAs will be limited in their capacity to transform their existing structures in order to free-up standing units to continue to sell services to schools, whether LMS or GM, in their own or other LEAs. There is evidence already to hand in fact that some LEAs are failing to win service contracts, particularly for cleaning and school meals (Anon, 1993a and David, 1993). Such developments have to be read in combination with the increasing reduction of the central budgets of LEAs as schools opt out of their control. Taken together, they point to a future in which LEAs, with reduced powers and funds, will find it very difficult to exert significant influence on the education services which, in days gone by, they helped to build up. Indeed, without significant financial discretion, it is unlikely that LEAs will be able to make policies that count, let alone place themselves in a position to encourage innovation within a service that has largely left them behind.

No doubt, most LEAs will try to respond to these challenges. Clearly, it is in their interest to discourage as many of their schools as possible from opting out in order to retain some control of their central budgets. Some, such as Leeds LEA, are prepared to delegate more than the government's LMS policy is asking. In other cases, LEAs have reorganized their services to make them more relevant and responsive to 'customer schools'. Thus, in Bromley, traditional primary, secondary and further education divisions have been reorganized into support, quality and monitoring departments. In nearly all LEAs, slimmed-down inspectorates have been trained to bid for, and undertake, contracts for the newly established national inspection of schools service. Other LEAs presently offer competitively priced payroll services to GM schools.

Moving in the direction of 'supplier LEAs' servicing 'customer schools' may provide some measure of protection. However, the future of the LEA is still in jeopardy, arising from a combination of pressures from three directions. First, the continued squeeze on all local authority services as the result of reductions in public sector expenditure generally. Second, the slimming down of their central services as more schools opt out. Third, the proposed abolition of education committees, which makes it difficult to defend education as a separate service. Indeed, in one particular LEA, Hillingdon, the future may have already arrived.

Over half of Hillingdon's secondary schools have opted out; the rest are either in the process of doing the same or keeping the idea under review. A £2 million cut in the education budget by a Conservative council committed to holding down the community charge triggered the exodus. In the present spending round, Hillingdon is expected to reduce its education expenditure by £4.2 million as part of its response to reduced central government grants (Beckett, 1993). Cost-cutting exercises in Hillingdon have included plans to reduce the number of teachers employed and the merging of the borough's social services and education departments.

How have these developments affected the management of education services in Hillingdon? In practical terms, its LEA is now responsible for primary education and for the provision of places for 'excluded' secondary school pupils and those with special education needs. Hillingdon is thus operating a minimalist education service. True, it fulfils its statutory duties, but it appears to do little else.

There are then a number of converging trends in education, reported in this and previous chapters, which suggest that many LEAs will be responsible, in the medium term, only for primary schools and provision of statutory services to secondary schools. While none of this is inevitable, the measures of the 1993 Education Act, coupled with what has already happened to LEAs in recent times, make it increasingly likely.

In a review of the White Paper proposals and their likely impact on LEAs, Cordingley and Kogan (1993) conclude that they will 'cause the LEA as a significant entity to wither away'. They argue that, without financial or substantial administrative resources, it is hard to envisage quite how local authorities will sustain meaningful relations with schools. Moreover, without LEAs providing the vital link between communities and schools, and between schools and central government, there remains the larger question of the principles on which education will be governed in the future. Since 1944, the education service has been governed via a series of checks and balances implicating and articulating the local and central state, with headteachers and the professional leadership of LEAs playing crucial roles. This will be replaced by a framework which provides for a rigorous separation of purchasers from providers. Thus schools will be encouraged to pursue vigorously their individual interests, while the FAS will be urged to go for maximum efficiency as the rationale of good governance. In effect, planning and democratic accountablity will be replaced by a model based on efficiency and atomization, structured around loosely coupled institutions overseen from the centre.

From aptitude to ability?

We noted in Chapter 1 that critics of opting out predicted, among other things, that it would be an instrument to bring back academically selective education by the backdoor. As we have argued elsewhere in this book, these fears have largely been unfounded. Those GM schools which have successfully applied for change of character have done so mainly on grounds other than to change their admissions policies in favour of selection by ability. In Chapter 1, however, we noted that the

DfE has given its approval to the idea that GM schools should be allowed to select a proportion of their intakes using the criteria of special aptitude in particular activities such as sport or music. We noted too a recent decision by the Education Secretary to permit one GM comprehensive school, Southlands School in Reading, to administer IQ and other tests in order to select and admit a 'fast stream'. Both developments have raised doubts about the government's long-term commitment to secondary comprehensive schooling.

For the supporters of comprehensive education, the situation may not be so bleak as it first appears. Southlands' change of admissions policy could be an idiosyncratic case, which has more to do with an initiative aimed at assisting it to survive, rather than being a herald of things to come (Hackett and Whitehead, 1993; Hughes, 1993). Other GM schools which have applied to become academically more selective have yet to have their applications decided. The long time that has lapsed since they were submitted may indicate ministerial caution, rather than any determination on the government's part to pursue the reintroduction of selection.

Issues for parents and governors

Schools and parents will be confronted by a variety of factors when asked to consider the option of seeking and supporting GM status. This section is not intended to be a catalogue of the presumed advantages and disadvantages of GM status, about which information may be gleaned from, among many other sources, the Association of Metropolitan Authorities (1992), the Advisory Centre for Education (1989), Local Schools Information and the GM Schools Centre. Rather, it seeks to identify some of the broad educational issues which will confront professionals and the general public as the proposals in the White Paper are taken forward into legislation.

The first concern must be the funding projections as they apply to GM schools. That GM schools will continue to enjoy a relative funding advantage over LEA-maintained schools is secured by the protected portion of the central budget which they receive in addition to their LMS-based entitlement. But, if the government's squeeze on public spending continues, this is bound to feed through into reductions to GM schools' budgets. This is already happening in Hillingdon and

Gloucestershire, with consequent problems for GM schools which, hitherto, had enjoyed enhanced staff complements (Anon, 1993). As Rogers (1993) observes:

> GM schools which ... used their inflated budgets to employ additional staff ... could be in serious difficulties. For once they have been GM for a year, they will be liable for the full, and often heavy cost of severance ... payments.

Schools considering opting out will also need to determine what the direct effects on their grants will be if they are located in an LEA which spends more than the centrally-determined SSA figure on education. Although transition arrangements will ensure that existing GM schools are not unduly affected by downward adjustments in their allocation of the central budget, new entrants to the sector may not be so protected. Given these uncertainties, schools wanting to opt out will need to do their financial calculations with some care.

The general area of school management has caused concern amongst existing GM heads. There is little in the White Paper that addresses directly the troubled area of the division of labour between governors and heads. The Stratford School affair, during which the head and her chair of governors came into direct conflict (Anon, 1992), may well be an exception to the general rule. Even so, it highlights the need for everyone involved to work out in advance what is entailed in managing and governing an autonomously incorporated school.

Under the new funding arrangements, the survival of all state schools will depend increasingly on their ability to recruit and retain pupils in numbers sufficient to preserve existing staff levels. However, as our research indicates, GM status alone does not stimulate greater parental interest or participation, nor is it a major factor influencing parents' choice of school. If schools consider opting out, therefore, they face some decisions about how best to market their reputations and secure and retain parental interest. Our research shows that a number of GM schools have taken steps to manage their reputations in ways that distinguish them from adjacent LEA schools, often via stricter uniform codes, tighter discipline and superior facilities. While, in the short term, many will undoubtedly have some success marketing themselves in this way, it may not be so easy for them as and when their main competitors within the LEA and private sectors strive to 'sell' their services with equal vigour. Moreover, as more schools opt out, the distinctiveness of 'being GM' will diminish. Accordingly, because there must always be losers in any local education market, GM schools, without a sympathetic LEA to help them through difficult times, may find the going hard as things settle down.

Without an LEA to advise on and monitor curricular and managerial matters, a GM school will need to consider how best to deploy and develop its existing staff, and how to maintain and further enhance the quality of the educational experiences on offer. It may well be that the experience of LMS has already prepared many schools for the increased responsibilities of GM status, but governing bodies will need to take a view on their school's existing capacity to assume further management and curriculum responsibilities in an increasingly competitive climate.

Governors and parents might be well advised to ask too whether GM status, in any event, is a necessary condition for school improvement. Put another way, are schools run on the principles of self-governance more likely to promote higher standards of attainment across the board than ones which choose to remain with the LEA? Chubb and Moe's (1992a, 1992b) recent reviews of the government's school reforms suggest they will, although the data for their claims seem to be derived from a very small and lightly researched sample of GM schools. GM status may well help some school managers to make more effective and efficient use of resources. But, as we indicated in Chapter 4, how this translates into increased levels of pupil motivation and achievement is less than clear. Moreover, as Levačić (1992) observes, many of the important factors said to be associated with school improvement – purposive leadership, positive school climate and the involvement of teachers in school decision-making – are not uniquely dependent on a high level of institutional autonomy. Indeed, the Rutter *et al.* (1979) and Mortimer *et al.* (1988) studies of secondary and junior education in Inner London, both of which pre-date the LMS and GM schools policies, indicate that self-governance may not be a necessary condition for school effectiveness.

Finally, there are signs that some governors and parents, particularly those associated with voluntary schools, think it important to ask and answer broadly-defined, moral questions about opting out. For example, does it promote more and better choices for everyone? Does it provide a pattern of educational governance that appeals to social cohesion? Is it proper for schools to make decisions on their futures without reference to their likely negative impact on neighbouring institutions? While the pursuit of answers to such questions is beyond the scope of this book, the issues they raise remain important. Certainly, they draw our attention away from an exclusive preoccupation with the techniques needed to manage self-governing schools towards the need to identify the values judged to be important in the provision of school services.

In this connection, our research does not permit us to reach firm conclusions about the contribution of GM schools to the creation of 'healthy' and 'fair' local education markets. On the other hand, our investigations in two selected areas, as reported in Chapter 6, suggest they have yet to extend significantly the choice of schools available to most parents. Moreover, as we indicate elsewhere, they have mostly acted to preserve the variety of schools from which they may choose. Accordingly, the suggestion that GM schools help to foster diversity and create new kinds of local education markets is not one our research is able to confirm. In any event, like Jonathan (1989), there may be cause to be justifiably sceptical of the government's implicit view that 'the welfare of each can be unproblematically aggregated to result in the welfare of all'. Such scepticism might also extend to a concern that, by privileging piecemeal rationality in the way envisaged by the GM schools policy, the government may not foster greater choice within the education market place but, rather, reproduce, even compound, the very inequalities which different groups of parents presently manifest in consuming the choices of school available to them (Young, 1992b).

Conclusion

The measures that we have have discussed in the foregoing sections will lead to a substantial increase in the central regulation of education at the expense of local accountability. The Education Secretary has assumed powers to intervene in unprecedented ways in the local planning and provision of education. Given the nature of these changes, coupled with our analysis in Chapter 4 of the work of GM heads, it is proper to ask if opted-out schools, in contrast to their LEA counterparts, are 'agents of the (central) state' (Naismith, 1992) in the sense that they must work *directly* to a remit imposed from the centre.

The National Curriculum policy constrains all schools, not just ones that have opted out, in terms of what they can teach. Ministers, however, have been increasingly willing to devise and support a range of initiatives aimed at expanding its technological aspects. Schools are also being encouraged to identify and develop areas of specialization compatible with their own interests and expertise. These local initiatives, however, must be approved, either by ministers or their nominees. In curriculum terms, therefore, the latitude GM schools have for innovation and diversity is limited and, to a greater degree than ever before, ministerially determined and regulated.

In view of the government's declared objectives, we need to ask, too, if opting out is likely to contribute to improvements in educational standards. Nothing in our data permits us to do much more than speculate about the relationship between increased autonomy for schools and increases in the levels of motivation and achievement of their pupils. In any event, the benefits which our headteacher respondents associate with GM status have more to do with enhanced levels of resources – input measures, in other words. Paradoxically, the government wishes to deny any such link between increased school expenditure and educational benefits. Undoubtedly, many GM schools have managed their affairs efficiently and in ways which have put more resources into classrooms. As the policy takes hold and implicates many more schools, this may have to be accomplished at a cost to adjacent schools whose incomes have to be reduced so that GM schools can continue to receive their protected share of the central budget. As the global sum available diminishes, it will require skilful management just to sustain existing levels of staff. Indeed, there is a strong likelihood that new entrants to the GM sector will find that increased managerial efficiency will no longer translate into surpluses which can be redeployed within subject departments or classrooms.

Nor is there any evidence that an increasing emphasis on competition between schools contributes to any increase in standards. True, as we discovered, it brings about a variety of renewed and innovative attempts at reputation management designed to maintain and increase levels of pupil recruitment. It also leads to attempts to resurrect 'traditional' educational imagery and associated practices. However, it is simplistic to interpret these, mostly surface, features as substantive changes in the quality of education provision.

Even so, the measures contained in the White Paper and 1993 Education Act hold out the interesting prospect of new schools being

THE POLICY'S LONG-TERM IMPLICATIONS

established which will be eligible for government support as GM institutions. While religious groups may be the first to enter the field, the opportunity also exists for other community groups to establish schools which might extend choice and diversity in education in unexpected ways. In the medium term, however, schools are more likely to be involved in exercises designed to ensure their continued existence, and within a framework where choice and diversity translate into competition for survival.

Appendix 1: Categories of Social Class

The categories of social class used in this book are derived from Hope-Goldthorpe (Goldthorpe and Hope, 1974). They are based on a ranking of the socio-economic status of occupation. These categories are as follows:

Service class
I Higher grade professionals, managers, etc, self-employed or salaried higher-grade administrators, officials in central/local government and public/private enterprises (including company directors), managers in large industrial establishments, large proprietors.
II Lower-grade professionals/administrators/officials, higher-grade technicians, managers in small business/industrial/service establishments, supervisors of non-manual workers.

Intermediate class
III Routine non-manual, mainly clerical, sales and rank-and-file employees in service.
IV Small proprietors, including farmers/smallholders/self-employed artisans/own-account workers other than professionals.
V Lower-grade technicians (whose work is to some extent manual), supervisors of manual workers.

Working class
VI Skilled manual wage-workers, all industries.
VII All manual wage-workers in semi- and unskilled grades, agricultural workers.

Appendix 2: Contact Addresses and Sources of Information

There are agencies, other than local education authorities and the major teacher organizations, that offer advice and information to schools, governors and parent groups that want to know more about grant-maintained status. These include:

Organizations

Choice in Education (36 Great Smith Street, London SW1P 3BU. Tel. 071-799 2660). This organization, which is directed by an active member of the Conservative Party, is both ideologically and educationally committed to the GM schools policy. Choice in Education campaigns on behalf of the policy and offers free literature and speakers for schools considering opting out.

The Grant Maintained Schools Centre (Wesley Court, 4a Priory Road, High Wycombe HP13 6SE. Tel. 0494 474470). This organization, like Choice in Education, supports the GM schools policy and is partly funded by government grant for this purpose. However, unlike Choice in Education, the Centre does not overtly campaign on behalf of the policy. Even so, the advice and information it offers spring from the conviction that opting out is a good thing. The Centre assists schools which seek GM status and provides services on a paid consultancy basis to those which eventually opt out.

Keep Our Schools Local is the name of a loosely coordinated network of parent groups that have been involved in campaigns to stop schools opting out in areas as far afield as Cambridgeshire, Leicestershire, Swindon and Huddersfield. For further information about Keep Our Schools Local contact: Angela Milroy, 3 Bellefield Crescent, Trowbridge BA14 8SR. Tel. 0225 763809.

Local Schools Information (11–13 Charterhouse Buildings, Goswell Road, London EC1M 7AN. Tel. 071-490 4942) is funded by trade unions and local authorities. While Local Schools Information claims to offer disinterested advice and information about opting out, its public pronouncements about the policy are often critical and occasionally oppositional. Like Choice in Education, it supplies speakers to schools contemplating opting out as well as free literature. It also operates a telephone information service.

Publications

For further information and research-based and critical analysis of opting out see the following publications:

Association of Metropolitan Authorities (1990) *Grant Maintained Schools: Independence or Isolation?* (London, AMA). This booklet discusses what is meant by GM status and examines some of the claims made for and against the decision to opt out.

Bush, T, Coleman, M and Glover, G (1993) *Managing Autonomous Schools: The Grant-Maintained Experience*, London: Paul Chapman. This book is based on independent research. Its five case studies, which include one on the first primary schools to opt out, offer helpful insights on how different institutions manage the transition from LEA-maintained to grant-maintained status.

Davies, B and Anderson, L (1992) *Opting for Self-Management: The Early Experience of Grant-Maintained Schools*, London: Routledge. This book is a mostly 'how-to' educational management text which offers practical advice about how to seek GM status and run an opted-out school. Although the authors' analysis of the policy is even-handed, the rest of the text derives from contributors, such as headteachers of GM schools, who are committed to opting out.

Grant-Maintained Schools Foundation (1992) *Governors and Heads in Grant-Maintained Schools*, Harlow: Longman. This book examines the relationship between school governors and heads in GM schools. It is an entirely 'how-to' guide which assumes uncritically the role of the head as 'chief executive of the school'.

Nobel, T and Wright, B (1993) *The Primary Perspective – The First Twelve Months*, Northampton: JEMA Publications. This slim volume, written by two GM primary headteachers, is a practical guide to opting out. It is the only text presently available on GM status which exclusively addresses the circumstances of opted-out primary schools. Its analysis, however, offers little criticism of the policy's rationale and its possible negative effects.

Office for Standards in Education (1993) *Grant-Maintained Schools 1989–92*, London: Her Majesty's Stationery Office. This report is about the standards and quality of education in GM schools. It is based on inspection evidence gathered from 81 GM schools (mostly secondaries) between September 1989 and July 1992.

Rogers, M (1992) *Opting Out: Choice and the Future of Schools*, London: Lawrence and Wishart. This book, authored by the coordinator of Local Schools Information, outlines the political origins of opting out and provides information to enable parents, teachers and governors to make informed choices about seeking GM status for their school. Although *Opting Out* is a mostly factual guide, its author sees 'little logic' in choosing to opt out.

Rogers, R (1989) *Considering the Options: A Guide to Opting Out*, London: Advisory Centre for Education. This booklet offers an analysis of the origins of opting out and factual information on the process of seeking GM status and the sorts of issues parents often seek clarification about once they hear of an opt-out plan. It also includes sections on campaigning and the ballot.

Sexton, S (1989) *Opting to Grant-Maintained Status*, London: Institute of Economic Affairs. This pamphlet, authored by one of the leading members of the neo-liberal wing of the New Right and published by one of its 'think tanks', provides both a practical guide to opting out and an ideological justification for seeking GM status. The booklet also includes a short section on the meaning of GM status written by the headteacher of one of the first secondary schools to opt out.

Government publications

Government publications on the GM schools policy include:

Grant-Maintained Schools: Experiences During the First Year (1992)
Grant-Maintained Schools: Funding Fact Sheet (1992)
Grant-Maintained Schools: Questions Parents Ask (1992)
Grant-Maintained Schools: Questions Staff Ask (1992)
School Governors: How to Become a Grant-Maintained School (1991)

These publications are available from the Department for Education Publications Despatch Centre, PO Box 2193, London E15 2EU. Tel. 081-533 2000.

Appendix 3: Glossary of Key Terms

Annual Maintenance Grant (AMG) The amount of money paid each year by the Department for Education (DfE) to GM schools to cover their day-to-day running costs. A school's AMG consists of three parts: (1) *direct AMG:* the amount of money it would get under its former LEA's LMS scheme; (2) *central AMG:* cash equivalent to the services formerly provided free by the LEA; (3) *meals AMG:* equivalent to the subsidies which the LEA pays per pupil for both free and paid meals.

Capital grants These are paid annually by the DfE to GM schools in two forms: (1) *formula allocations:* grants of £10,000 per school plus £20 per pupil for small capital projects such as building alterations and improvements; (2) *named projects:* grants for specific, larger-scale projects for which GM schools bid.

Change of character Local authority and GM schools may only be enlarged significantly (usually by 20 per cent or more), take children of different ages or begin or cease to select pupils by ability with the assent of the Education Secretary. Such changes are known as 'changing the character of the school' and require public consultation.

Common Funding Formula (CFF) Based largely on pupil numbers, the CCF will be overseen by the Funding Agency for Schools and eventually provide a national formula for funding GM schools.

Comprehensive school A secondary school which does not select children for admission on the grounds of ability.

GRANT-MAINTAINED SCHOOLS

Funding Agency for Schools (FAS) A product of the 1993 Education Act, this body will eventually be responsible for administering GM schools (see Chapter 7 for details).

Grammar school A secondary school which only admits children of high academic ability selected at 11 years of age on the basis of test results.

Incorporation Schools run by the LEA are not legal entities in their own right, but part of that authority. However, when schools opt out they become a legal entity known as a corporation and, as such, can enter into contracts and be sued.

Local education authority (LEA) Part of the local government structure responsible for the provision and day-to-day running of the state education service in a particular geographical area.

Local Management of Schools (LMS) A measure in the 1988 Education Reform Act which requires LEAs to delegate funds to schools which they control by means of a weighted, per capita formula.

Special Purpose Grants (SPG) These are paid annually to GM schools and are of four kinds: (1) *SPG development:* a sum of money equivalent to that paid to LEAs for such things as staff training and implementing the National Curriculum; (2) *SPG premises:* a sum of money paid towards the cost of premises insurance based on schools' bids; (3) *SPG restructuring:* a one-off grant that GM schools can bid for to help with the cost of early retirements or redundancies; (4) *SPG VAT:* compensation for the fact that LEA-maintained schools can recover VAT on their spending but GM schools cannot.

Standard Spending Assessment (SSA) The sum of money that the government calculates a local authority needs to spend to provide a standard level of service.

Statementing The procedure leading to the identification of the special educational needs (SEN) of a child who needs more help than can be provided within the ordinary resources of a school.

GLOSSARY OF TERMS

Transitional Grant A one-off payment made to a school after it has been approved for GM status but not yet incorporated, it is designed to help ease the transition from being an LEA to an opted-out institution.

Voluntary schools Schools run by LEAs in conjunction with bodies such as the Church of England and the Roman Catholic Church.

References

Advisory Centre for Education (1989) *Considering the Options: A Guide to Opting Out*, London: Advisory Centre for Education.

Anon (1988) 'Baker still opting out of Thatcher camp', *Education*, 1 April.

Anon (1992) 'Preventing school fiefdoms', *The Independent*, 22 February.

Anon (1993) 'Opt-out jobs in jeopardy', *Times Educational Supplement*, 26 February.

Anon (1993a) 'Authorities fail to win GM contracts,' *Times Educational Supplement*, 15 January.

Arnott, M, Bullock, A and Thomas, H (1992) 'Consequences of local management: an assessment by headteachers', paper presented to the Eighth Education Reform Act Research Network Seminar, University of Warwick, February.

Association of County Councils (1988) 'Response to the Consultation Paper', in Haviland, J, (ed.) *Take Care! Mr Baker*, London: Fourth Estate.

Association of Metropolitan Authorities (1988) 'Response to the Consultation Paper', in Haviland, J, (ed.) *Take Care! Mr Baker*, London: Fourth Estate.

Association of Metropolitan Authorities (1992) *Grant-Maintained Schools: Independence or Isolation?* London: Association of Metropolitan Authorities.

Audit Commission (1988) 'Response to the Consultation Paper', in Haviland, J, (ed.) *Take Care! Mr Baker*, London: Fourth Estate.

Audit Commission (1989) *Losing an Empire, Finding a Role: The LEA of the Future*, London: Her Majesty's Stationery Office.

REFERENCES

Baker, K (1988) 'Parliamentary Debates', *Proceedings of the House of Commons*, Col. 437, 23 March.

Ball, S J (1992a) 'Changing management and the management of change: educational reform and school processes', paper presented at the Annual Conference of the American Educational Research Association, San Francisco, April.

Ball, S J (1992b) 'Schooling, enterprise and the market', paper presented at the Annual Conference of the American Educational Research Association, San Francisco, April.

Ball, S J (1992c) 'The worst of three possible worlds: policy, power relations and teachers' work', keynote address to the British Educational Management and Administration Society's Research Conference, University of Nottingham, April.

Ball, S J, Gewirtz, S and Bowe, R (1992) 'What's in an open evening/day?' Paper presented at the Parental Choice and Market Forces Seminar 2, King's College, London, 31 January.

Bates, S (1991) 'Major admits opt-out schools get extra to encourage the others', *The Guardian*, 7 August.

Beckett, F (1993) 'A dream for some, a nightmare for others', *The Guardian*, 9 February.

Blackburne, L (1992) 'Selection ruling opens back door', *Times Educational Supplement*, 6 November.

Bogdanov, V (1992) 'Heading for square one?', *Times Educational Supplement*, 6 November.

Bowe, R and Ball, S J (with Gold, R) (1992) *Reforming Education and Changing Schools: Case Studies in Policy Sociology*, London: Routledge.

Bowe, R, Ball, S J and Gewirtz, S (1992) 'What's in a prospectus?', paper presented at The Parental Choice and Market Forces Seminar 2, King's College, University of London, 31 January.

Brent Local Education Authority (1988) 'Response to the Consultation Paper', in Haviland, J, (ed.) *Take Care! Mr Baker*, London: Fourth Estate.

Brighouse, T (1989) 'Dodgy cocktails', *Times Educational Supplement*, 23 June.

Brown, S and Baker, L (1992) *About Change: Schools' and LEAs' Perspectives on LEA Reorganization*, Windsor: National Foundation for Educational Research.

Bush, T and Coleman, M (1992) *The Financial Implications of Mass*

Opting Out, Northampton: Educational Management Development Unit, University of Leicester.
Chanan, G (1987) 'No option', *Times Educational Supplememt*, 24 July.
Chubb, J E and Moe, T M (1992a) 'How to get the best from Britain's schools', *The Sunday Times Magazine*, 9 February, 18–36.
Chubb, J E and Moe, T M (1992b) *A Lesson in School Management from Great Britain*, Washington DC: The Brookings Institution.
Conservative Party (1992) *Better Schools, Better Standards*, London: Conservative and Unionist Central Office.
Cordingley, P and Kogan, M (1993) *In Support of Education: The Functioning of Local Government*, London: Jessica Kingsley.
Cormack, P (1988) 'Parliamentary Debates', *Proceedings of the House of Commons*, Col. 437, 23 March.
Cox, C B and Boyson, R (1975) *Black Paper 1975*, London: Dent.
Cox, C B and Boyson, R (1977) *Black Paper 5*, London: Temple Smith.
Cox, C B and Dyson, A E (1969a) *The Crisis in Education*, London: The Critical Quarterly Society.
Cox, C B and Dyson, A E (1969b) *The Fight for Education*, London: The Critical Quarterly Society.
Dale, R (1989) 'Education and the capitalist state: contributions and contradictions', in Dale, R *The State and Education Policy*, Milton Keynes: Open University Press.
Dale, R (1992) 'What do they know of England who don't know they are speaking prose', paper presented to the ESRC Seminar, Methodological and Ethical Issues Associated with Research into the 1988 Education Reform Act, University of Warwick, 29 April.
David, T (1993) 'Who buys what?' *Education*, 5 March.
Davies, B and Anderson, L (1992) *Opting for Self-Management: The Early Experience of Grant-Maintained Schools*, London: Routledge.
Dearlove, J and Saunders, P (1991) *Introduction to British Politics*, Cambridge: Polity Press.
Deem, R and Wilkins, J (1992) 'Governing and managing schools after ERA: the LEA experience and the GMS alternative', in Simkins, T, Ellison, L and Garrett, V (eds) *Implementing Educational Reform: The Early Lessons*, London: Longman.
Department of Education and Science (1987) *Grant-Maintained Schools: Consultative Paper*, London: DES.
Department of Education and Science (1991) *Grant-Maintained Schools: Experiences During the First Year*, London: DES.

REFERENCES

Department of Education and Science (1992) *Education in England 1990–91: The Annual Report of HM Chief Inspector of Schools*, London: Her Majesty's Stationery Office.

Department for Education (1992a) *Choice and Diversity: A New Framework for Schools*, London: Her Majesty's Stationery Office.

Department for Education (1992b) *A Common Funding Formula for Schools*, London: DfE.

Department for Education (1992c) 'Funding proposals for grant-maintained schools in 1993–94', *Department for Education News*, 387/92, 24 November.

Department for Education (1992d) 'Merton's Director of Education asked about opt-out campaign at Rutlish School', *Department for Education News*, 422/9, 22 December.

Edwards, T, Fitz, J and Whitty, G (1989) *The State and Private Education: An Evaluation of the Assisted Places Scheme*, London: Falmer Press.

Edwards, T, Gewirtz, S and Whitty, G (1992) 'City technology colleges and curriculum innovation', paper presented at The Parental Choice and Market Forces Seminar 2, King's College, University of London, 31 January.

Edwards, T and Whitty, G (1992) 'Parental choice and educational reform in Britain and the United States', *British Journal of Educational Studies*, **40**, 2, 101–17.

Efficiency Unit (1988) *Improving Management in Government: The Next Steps*, London: Her Majesty's Stationery Office.

Fairhall, J (1985) 'Thatcher wants direct grant schools', *The Guardian*, 18 July.

Fisher, A (1987) 'Fears for the future of the "forgotten" children', *Times Educational Supplement*, 6 November.

Fitz, J and Halpin, D (1991) 'From a sketchy policy to a workable scheme: grant-maintained schools and the Department of Education and Science', *International Studies in Sociology of Education*, **1**, 129–52.

Fletcher, N (1988) 'Mets bounce back with closure warnings', *Education*, 25 November.

Flude, M and Hammer, M (1990) 'Opting into an uncertain future: grant-maintained schools', in Flude, M and Hammer, M (eds) *The Education Reform Act: Its Origins and Implications*, London: Falmer Press.

Garner, R (1987) 'Mrs Thatcher enthuses over opting-out proposals', *Times Educational Supplement*, 18 September.

Gewirtz, S, Whitty, G and Edwards, T (1992) 'City technology colleges: schooling for the Thatcher generation', *British Journal of Educational Studies*, **40**, 3, 207–17.

Gill, N (1989) 'Press report', *The Independent*, 23 February.

Gilmour, I (1992) *Dancing with Dogma*, London: Simon & Schuster.

Goldthorpe, J and Hope, K (1974) *The Social Grading of Occupations*, Oxford: Clarendon Press.

Grant Maintained Schools Centre (1991) *Annual Report*, High Wycombe: Grant Maintained Schools Centre.

Grant Maintained Schools Centre (1992a), *Annual Report*, High Wycombe: Grant Maintained Schools Centre.

Grant Maintained Schools Centre (1992b) *The Standing Advisory Committee for Grant Maintained Schools*, High Wycombe: Grant Maintained Schools Centre.

Gretton, J and Jackson, M (1976) *William Tyndale: Collapse of a System or a School?* London: George Allen & Unwin.

Hackett, G (1993) 'Opt-out bodies too close for comfort', *Times Educational Supplement*, 26 February.

Hackett, G and Whitehead, M (1993) 'Ministers step softly on selection', *Times Educational Supplement*, 19 February.

Halpin, D and Fitz, J (1990) 'Researching grant-maintained schools', *Journal of Education Policy*, **5**, 2, 167–80.

Harding, R (1987) 'Careering off down the wrong road', *Times Educational Supplement*, 3 July.

Haviland, J (ed.) (1988) *Take Care, Mr Baker!*, London: Fourth Estate.

Hillgate Group (1986) *Whose Schools? A Radical Manifesto*, London: Claridge Press.

Hodges, L (1985) 'Government takes a fresh look at schools plan', *The Times*, 18 July.

Horn, J (1987) 'Diving into dangerous waters', *Times Educational Supplement*, 18 December.

Hughes, C (1993) 'Comprehensive school allowed to select on ability', *The Independent*, 16 February.

Hugill, B (1987) 'Bishops move – but which way?', *Times Educational Supplement*, 27 November.

Hunter, P (1987) 'The false premises behind the Conservative proposals on opting out', *Education*, 19 June.

REFERENCES

Hymas, C (1993) 'Patten increases opt-out pressure', *The Sunday Times*, 31 January.

Jonathan, R (1989) 'Choice and control in education: parental rights and social justice', *British Journal of Educational Studies*, **37**, 4, 321–38.

Judd, J (1993) 'Charity for schools is Tory Front', *The Independent*, 12 January.

Kemp, P (1990) 'Next steps for the British civil service', *Governance*, **3**, 2, 186–96.

Kickert, W (1991) 'Steering at a distance: a new paradigm of public governance in Dutch higher education', paper for the European Consortium of Political Research, University of Essex, March.

Last, E H (1987) 'Small schools will suffer if opt-out plans go through', *Times Educational Supplement*, 11 December, 20.

Levačić, R (1992) 'Local management of schools: aims, scope and impact', *Journal of Educational Management and Administration*, **20**, 1, 16–29.

Lodge, B (1987) 'Clergy fears opting out will close its schools', *Times Educational Supplement*, 20 November.

MacGregor, J (1990) *Conservative Party Conference News*, 10 October, London: Conservative Party Central Office.

Maclure, S (1988) *Education Re-formed: A Guide to the Education Reform Act*, London: Hodder & Stoughton.

Maclure, S (1992) 'Buy my pig in a poke', *Times Educational Supplement*, 4 September.

Meickle, J (1987) 'Opt-out plan casts doubt on maintained sector', *Times Educational Supplement*, 29 May.

Mortimore, P, Sammons, P, Stoll, L, Lewos, D and Ecob, R (1988) *School Matters*, Wells: Open Books.

Naismith, D (1992) 'Education and choice in Britain', keynote address given at the Institute of Economic Affairs/Manhattan Institute Conference, Education and Choice in Britain and the USA, Royal Society of Arts, London, 17 November.

Nash, I and Garner, R (1987) 'Baker quiets fears of mass opt-out', *Times Educational Supplement*, 18 September.

Nobel, T and Wright, B (1992) *Grant-Maintained Status: The Primary Perspective*, Northampton: JEMA Publications.

No Turning Back Group of MPs (1986) *Save Our Schools*, London: Conservative Political Centre.

Parkes, S (1987) 'Opting out may hurt special needs pupils', *Times Educational Supplement*, 23 November.

Passmore, B (1985) 'Thatcher hints at return to direct grant grammar schools', *Times Educational Supplement*, 19 July.

Pyke, N (1993) 'Double pay-off for the opted-out', *Times Educational Supplement*, 12 February.

Ranson, S (1990) *The Politics of Reorganizing Schools*, London: Unwin Hyman.

Ranson, S (1991) 'Notes towards a data set and a theory of emergent local systems of education', paper presented to the Annual Conference of the British Educational Management and Administration Society, University of Leeds, September.

Ranson, S (1992) 'LEA responses to the Education Reform Act', in Simkins, T, Ellison, L and Garrett, V (eds) *Implementing Educational Reform: The Early Lessons*, London: Longman.

Ridley, N (1992) *My Style of Government*, London, Fontana.

Rogers, M (1992) *Opting Out: Choice and the Future of Schools*, London: Lawrence & Wishart.

Rogers, M (1993) 'How a bribe can backfire', *Education*, 19 February.

Rumbold, A (1989) 'Parliamentary Debates', *Proceedings of the House of Commons*, Col. 337, 3 March.

Rutter, M, Maughan, B, Mortimore, P and Ouston, J (1979) *Fifteen Thousand Hours*, London: Open Books.

Sexton, S (1987) *Our Schools: A Radical Policy*, Warlingham: Institute of Economic Affairs.

Society of Education Officers (1988) 'Response to the Consultation Paper', in Haviland, J (ed.) *Take Care! Mr Baker*, London: Fourth Estate.

Stewart, J (1992) 'The rebuilding of public accountability', paper presented at the European Policy Forum Conference, Accountability to the Public, London, December.

Sutcliffe, J (1987) 'Tory shires worried by opting-out threat', *Times Educational Supplement*, 4 December.

Tebbit, N (1987) 'Parliamentary Debates', *Proceedings of the House of Commons*, Col. 812, 1 December.

Thomas, G (1987) 'Opting out? No thanks', *Times Educational Supplement*, 11 December.

Thompson, M (1992) 'The experience of going grant-maintained: the perceptions of AMMA teacher representatives', *Journal of Teacher Development*, **1**, 3, 133–40.

Travers, T (1993) 'Postgraduate arithmetic', *Times Educational Supplement*, 15 January.

Walford, G and Miller, H (1991) *City Technology College*, Buckingham: Open University Press.

Wallace, R (1990) 'The Act and local authorities', in Flude, M and Hammer, M (eds) *The Education Reform Act: Its Origins and Implications*, London: Falmer Press.

Wilkins, J (1992) Private correspondence with the authors, 6 March.

Young, S (1992a) 'True blues refuse to toe the line', *Times Educational Supplement*, 6 November.

Young, S (1992b) 'Choice widens class divide', *Times Educational Supplement*, 12 October.

Index

academic selection 31, 105, 111–12
accountability 10, 67, 103–5
admissions policies 31, 43, 46, 111, 112
Advisory Centre for Education 112
Assisted Places Scheme (APS) 21, 24
Association of County Councils 51–2
Association of Metropolitan Authorities 50, 101, 112
Audit Commission 49, 51, 52

balloting for opting out 35, 108
Black Paper 19, 20
budgets 10, 107, 112, 113

capital allocation 29, 65
capital expenditure 30
Chief Education Officer 103
City Technology Colleges (CTCs) 24
Common Funding Formula (CFF) 106

community charge 110
Conservative Party 20, 24, 25, 32
consultation documents 25
consultation period 11, 49–52
customer schools 110

Department of Education and Science (DES) 19, 25, 26
DfE 31, 70, 102, 106, 107
Direct Grant Regulations 18
direct-grant schools 18
Director of Education 103
diversity of school provision 12

Education Act 1944 103
Education Act 1993 60, 102, 103, 108, 111, 116–17
education expenditure 110
education planning 103, 104
Education Reform Act 1988 9, 18, 24, 27
Education Reform Bill 1988 11, 22, 25, 26
educational opportunity 73

educational standards 13–14, 19, 23, 73, 75–6
entry point 102
exit point 103

financial benefits 72, 106
financial implications 51–2, 58–60, 64, 70, 113
financial incentives 35
first choice realization 81–2, 88–92
Funding Agency for Schools (FAS) 101–5
  composition of 104
  critical commentary on 103–4
  relationship with local communities 104
  unresolved difficulties 104
funding arrangements 29, 30, 42, 105–7, 113
funding parity 29–30
funding projections 112

government agencies 14
government commitments 20, 24
government hostility 22
government policy 17, 48
government support and encouragement 11
government thinking 75
governors
  of GM schools 67–70
  implications for 112–15
grammar schools 11, 43, 46
grant-maintained schools
  advantages of 64
  change of character 31, 85, 102, 111
  chief reason cited for seeking status of 63
  distinguishing features 9–10, 113–14
  distribution of 38
  diversity of 76
  factors influencing move towards 63–71
  geographical spread 39
  improvements in 93–4
  legal basis 9
  number of establishments involved 33–4
  parents and pupils as 'choosers' 77–82
  parents and pupils as 'users' 82–4
  policy conclusions 15–16
  policy direction 30
  policy modifications 28–31
  policy objectives 22–4
  policy origins 18–22
  regulated autonomy 70–71
  research conclusions 15–16
  specialization 31
  transition arrangements 113
  types of schools involved 43
  types of secondary school 43–6
  see also headteachers; opting out
Grant Maintained Schools Centre (GMSC) 77–8, 85, 101, 112
Grant Maintained Schools Trust 28

headteachers 61–74
  freedom of 71
  interviews with 61–2
  reactions to former LEAs 64–5
  role in seeking GM status 65–6

INDEX

Ibbs Report 13
independent schools 24, 91–3, 97
individualist emphasis of opting out 64–5
innovative projects 73
Institute of Economic Affairs 22
IQ tests 112

Labour Party 101
LEAs 9–12, 20, 22–4, 26, 28–30, 32, 34, 35, 38–40, 42, 43
   actual experience of opted-out schools 52–60
   finance and opted-out schools 58–60
   functions redefined 49
   future of 108–11
   impact of opting out on 48–60
   incremental demise of 103
   problems facing 109
   proposed relinquishment of planning functions 103
   reaction to draft proposals 50
   reactions of GM school heads to 64–5
   relations with opted-out schools 56–8
   reorganization plans 53–6, 78
   strategic planning 53–6
   supplier 110
   views on opting out 49–50
   weakening of present role of 108
local education authorities *see* LEAs
Local Management of Schools (LMS) scheme 10, 26, 32, 35, 107, 110, 112, 114
Local Schools Information 112

long-term implications 100–117

market competitiveness 23
market-led approaches 10
marketing issues 113
markets 86–99, 115
micro-markets 86–8
moral questions 114

National Curriculum 26, 27, 70, 73
negative responses 11, 26, 49–50
New Right 19, 22–5, 27
No Turning Back Group 22

open days/evenings 93
opting out
   advantages of 71–2, 75
   contrast between Labour and Conservative LEAs 40–41
   distribution of 38–43
   domino effect 39
   formulating 24–8
   impact on LEAs 48–60
   implementing 24–8
   individualist emphasis of 64–5
   initiating process 9
   legal basis 9
   measures designed to remove particular barriers to further progress in scale and pace of 107
   misinformation on 41
   pace of 34–5
   patterns of 33–47
   policy 11
   prime-movers in process of 65–6
   reasons for 35

opting out (cont.)
  research project 14–16
  scale of 33
  and school closures 35–8
  uneven impact of 42
  see also grant-maintained schools

parent action groups 66–7
parent interviews 77
parental accountability 23
parental choice 11, 12, 21, 24, 51, 75, 76, 81–2, 86, 90
parental participation 83
parental power 75
parental views 12
parents
  as choosers of GM schools 77–82
  as GM school users 82–4
  implications for 112–15
primary schools 43, 108
Prime Minister's Policy Unit 25
private sector 21, 75, 91
prospectuses 93
public sector institutions, self-managing 13
public sector reorganization 13–14
pupils
  achievement 73
  as GM school choosers 77–82
  as GM school users 82–4
  interviews with 76
  perceptions of opting out 95–7

'quality' schooling 12–13

religious bodies 105

reputation management 93–5
reservations 12

school closures 35–8, 50, 55, 104
school image 94
school reorganization 38, 50, 53–6, 78
school uniform 93, 95
secondary schools 43–6
selection *see* academic selection
social class 91–3
  categories of 118
Society of Education Officers 50, 52
socio-economic status 92
specialization in education 105
Standing Advisory Committee (Headteachers) for Grant Maintained Schools (SAC) 62
Standard Spending Assessment (SSA) 106
statutory services to secondary schools 111

teaching staff of GM schools 68–9
Technology Schools Initiative (TSI) 31
transitional awards 107
two-tier system of education 76

voluntary schools 114
vouchers 21–2, 24

White Paper, *Choice and Diversity: A New Framework for Schools* 12, 31, 75, 100–108, 116–17
William Tyndale Junior School 19